Praise for *Unlocking Innovation*

"Ideas? Easier than ever. Leading innovation? Trickier than ever... unless you've got this book."
MICHAEL BUNGAY STANIER, author of *The Coaching Habit*

"Robyn M. Bolton's insights on building an innovation culture that thrives within existing corporate structures are spot-on. *Unlocking Innovation* is an invaluable resource for anyone navigating corporate innovation, providing a relatable and human-centered framework while emphasizing the importance of leadership behavior, smart structures, and a supportive culture. It is the playbook every CXO needs to drive meaningful change and deliver measurable impact."
BEN GEHEB, global chief experience (CX) strategy officer at VML

"Robyn M. Bolton's book stands out for its practical, nuts-and-bolts approach to innovation. As an executive, I appreciate how she anticipates the real-world challenges we face over time and provides concrete strategies to overcome them. This is the kind of book you can hand to a new innovation leader and say 'make it so.'"
JOERN KALLMEYER, chief supply chain officer at tms

"In *Unlocking Innovation*, Robyn M. Bolton offers a rare combination of sharp insight and wit to successfully drive innovation. Her examples deeply resonate with my experiences in biotech, providing the kind of practical wisdom that can accelerate breakthrough discoveries and their path to market."
RACHEL SHA, CEO of Vaxess Technologies

"The cupboard was bare. After the innovation pipeline had been mismanaged for several years, I was asked to take over and start from scratch. It was the first time in my career we literally had no new products in development. The VP of R&D and I, then VP of strategic marketing, embraced a new approach to jump-start innovation. Our added challenge was building new teams at the same time. With the clock ticking, and the business desperate for new platforms, we called in help, which came in the form of Robyn M. Bolton. Working with her, we transformed the mindsets of both marketing and R&D and unleashed our creativity. We moved through concepts quickly, based on consumer insights, and then accelerated development with the toolkit and coaching she provided. The result? We launched a pipeline that produced new revenue for over a decade, including the number-one-selling glucose meter in the world."

ERIC COMPTON, former president and CEO

"One of the toughest things for companies is to build the foundation for effective innovation over time. Too often, they want the shiny innovation skyscraper, without spending time on the foundation. And that leads to disaster. *Unlocking Innovation* provides a pragmatic three-year guide to setting innovation initiatives up for real, enduring success. Robyn M. Bolton learned with one of the greats—the late Clayton Christensen—and in this book she builds on many of his most important principles."

SCOTT KIRSNER, CEO and cofounder of InnoLead

"I know from experience that Robyn M. Bolton is a masterfully adept practitioner of innovation. I'm thrilled that she has captured her insights and approach in a book that will let readers benefit from her thinking—just as my colleagues and I did."

CHARLES BEST, CEO of Lakeshore Learning and founder of DonorsChoose

"*Unlocking Innovation* easily conveys what it takes to lead a team and organization to create 'something new that creates value' in the world. Robyn M. Bolton deftly details the path and challenges to successfully innovating in big companies."

BETSY FROST, CEO of Hoplark

"In *Unlocking Innovation*, Robyn M. Bolton cuts through the noise with practical, mission-driven advice for leaders. Her framework for building behavior, architecture, and culture aligns perfectly with the challenges of innovating in purpose-driven organizations like education technology."

ROB WALDRON, chairman of Curriculum Associates, Inc.

"Corporate leaders who are serious about making innovation a priority will be more likely to succeed if they understand the principles explained in this book. Meaningful innovation is hard; Robyn M. Bolton teaches how to make it attainable."

ELLIOTT PARKER, CEO of High Alpha Innovation

"*Unlocking Innovation* is an essential playbook for leaders aiming to bridge the gap between ambitious ideas and meaningful innovation. Robyn M. Bolton's approach goes beyond surface-level discussions of vision and culture and delves into the practical steps required to embed innovation within an organization."

NINA HUNTEMANN, chief academic officer of Chegg

"As someone who has been in the trenches of corporate innovation, I can attest to the power of Robyn M. Bolton's insights. *Unlocking Innovation* is a must-read for anyone looking to build a culture of innovation that thrives within the constraints of established organizations."

BRIAN ARDINGER, author of *Accelerated: The Guide to Innovating at the Speed of Change*

UNLOCKING
INNOVATION

ROBYN M. BOLTON

UNLOCKING

A LEADER'S GUIDE FOR
TURNING BOLD IDEAS
INTO TANGIBLE RESULTS

INNOVATION

PAGE TWO

Cataloguing in publication information is
available from Library and Archives Canada.
ISBN 978-1-77458-561-0 (paperback)
ISBN 978-1-77458-568-9 (ebook)

Page Two
pagetwo.com

Edited by James Harbeck
Copyedited by Crissy Boylan
Proofread by Alison Strobel
Cover, interior design, and illustrations by Taysia Louie

MileZero.io

For Matt

Contents

Foreword by
Dr. Marshall Goldsmith

IN TODAY'S rapidly evolving business landscape, innovation is no longer a luxury—it's a necessity. Organizations that fail to innovate risk being left behind, unable to compete in a world that thrives on the next big idea. Yet innovation is often misunderstood. It's not merely about coming up with a groundbreaking idea; it's about transforming that idea into a tangible result that adds value. Robyn M. Bolton's *Unlocking Innovation* is a master class in navigating this complex journey from concept to reality.

Robyn brings a wealth of experience and insight to this subject, having spent years in the trenches of corporate innovation. Her unique perspective is shaped by her extensive experience working with top executives and innovation teams. This book is not just a theoretical exploration; it's also a practical guide that distills the lessons Robyn has learned from real-world successes and failures. She challenges the traditional notion that innovation is solely about ideation, emphasizing instead that it's about execution and the willingness to take risks, make decisions, and push boundaries.

Unlocking Innovation is structured around a holistic framework that covers all aspects of leading innovation within an organization.

Robyn meticulously lays out the ABCs of Innovation—a clear, actionable road map that leaders can follow to foster a culture of creativity and drive impactful change. This framework is about more than just strategy; it's about building a sustainable ecosystem where innovation can thrive. This book teaches the crucial element that true innovation leaders are those who see beyond immediate challenges, who can envision a future, and who can rally their teams to bring that vision to life.

What sets this book apart is its emphasis on the human element of innovation. Robyn addresses the fears and uncertainties that often accompany bold ideas. She acknowledges that choosing to innovate is inherently risky, both for individuals and for organizations. But she also makes a compelling case for why the rewards far outweigh the risks. By framing innovation as a choice between safety and growth, Robyn empowers leaders to embrace uncertainty and to view it not as a threat, but as an opportunity to redefine what's possible.

As you begin on this journey through *Unlocking Innovation*, prepare to be challenged, inspired, and equipped with the tools you need to turn bold ideas into reality. Robyn doesn't just tell you what needs to be done—she shows you how to do it, guiding you every step of the way. Whether you're a seasoned executive or a new leader looking to make a mark, this book will provide you with the insights and strategies needed to lead your organization into a future shaped by innovation. The path ahead may not always be easy, but as Robyn shows us, it's the path that leads to true transformation.

DR. MARSHALL GOLDSMITH is the Thinkers50 number one executive coach and *New York Times*-bestselling author of *The Earned Life*, *Triggers*, and *What Got You Here Won't Get You There*.

What's the Problem?

CONGRATULATIONS! You have the awesome privilege and responsibility of growing your organization by creating new things that deliver impact. Or, as your boss or HR rep said, you are leading innovation.

Whether you volunteered for this role or were volun-told that it was yours, you are at the start of an exciting journey that changes you, your teams, your organizations, and maybe even your industry and the world. Like all great journeys, it will be perilous because you will confront challenges, obstacles, and heartbreak beyond what you can imagine. Like all great heroes, I believe that you will be victorious in the end. But before we pack up and set out, you need to know where you are and what you're up against.

In 1997, *The Innovator's Dilemma* was published. Though it wasn't the first book on innovation, it plucked innovation out of inventors' minds and scientists' labs and flung it onto CEOs' agendas and into popular business discourse.

CEOs scrambled to avoid the mistakes Clayton Christensen outlined in his doctoral-thesis-turned-bestseller. Paranoid about possible disruptors and deeply skeptical that their teams had the creativity or courage to innovate, executives hired consultants, devoured books and articles on the topic, and installed new frameworks and tools. As the innovation industrial complex grew, terms like "design thinking," "human-centered design," and "lean startup" became commonplace, and innovation teams, corporate venture capital, venture studios, hackathons, and accelerator programs spread like wildfire.

Yet decades later, the results of corporate innovation efforts haven't changed.

- 0.1 percent of ideas developed by companies launch

- 5 percent of launched products are still on the market a year later

- Less than 50 percent of these launched ideas achieve $1 million in sales

That means that only 0.002 percent of incubated ideas generate $1 million or more in revenue.

What is different about the journey of the 0.002 percent that enabled them to defy the odds?

I've asked this question most of my career, including during the nine years I spent at the consulting firm founded by Clayton Christensen, the author of the book that started it all. Only recently did I realize I had been given the answer before I thought to ask the question.

My first job after graduating from Miami University was as an assistant brand manager at Procter & Gamble. Everyone told me how lucky I was to land a job at such an iconic company, especially since it was the one that essentially created the concept of brand marketing. I did not share this sentiment. I dreamed of working at an advertising agency where I could be creative and push boundaries. I didn't think that could happen at a stodgy, insular, old-school company like P&G. But P&G paid twice what the advertising agencies paid and was in a city that cost half as much to live in, so practicality won out, and I took the job.

I was right to take the job. I was so very wrong about what was possible there.

A mere nine months after starting my job, I was part of the team announcing the North American launch of Swiffer. The moment onstage in Orlando, in front of P&G's North American sales force, was exhilarating and more than made up for the scars I earned battling agencies, debating in corporate conference rooms, and navigating budgets and timelines. Not to mention the myriad of other challenges that college didn't prepare me for, like dealing with lice-infested yak hair for product demos or corporate spies on flights to our test market.

Today, Swiffer is a $1 billion brand and one of P&G's most well-known products. What people don't know is that it was mere moments away from being among the 99.9 percent of ideas that never launch. Swiffer survived not only because it was a great idea but also because a great leader took a massive risk.

Your Problem

Innovation is not an idea problem. It is a leadership problem.

If you ask most corporate executives why their companies' innovation efforts struggle to achieve results, they'll tell you that the problem is a lack of ideas or not enough big ideas.

They're wrong.

Every organization I've ever worked with is full of ideas. Every day, people see opportunities for improvement, are inspired by something they see in the market, or have zany ideas that just might work. But they don't share these ideas because they don't think anyone listens, they've shared ideas before only to be told to focus on their day jobs, or they're afraid of the repercussions of stepping outside their defined role and responsibility. People don't share ideas because someone somewhere in your organization made it clear that ideas weren't welcome.

The silencing of ideas is a problem. Especially if you believe that your organization needs ideas to improve and grow. But most managers, in their heart of hearts, are scared of the financial, operational, and even strategic risks that are inherent in new ideas. They know that if they play it safe, they'll hit their numbers, earn their bonuses, and get a promotion. Why risk all that on an idea that may not be good, probably isn't big enough, and almost certainly wouldn't generate results?

This is your problem.

As risky as innovation is for an organization, it's also risky personally and professionally.

In 2019, InnoLead, an organization specializing in supporting and studying corporate innovation, researched corporate innovators' careers. It found that the average tenure of someone working in corporate innovation was 4.4 years. Vice presidents of innovation had the longest tenure at 5.4 years, while managers and principals had the shortest at 3.3 years.

Those tenures aren't surprising when you learn that 90 percent of corporate innovation labs and incubators fail within three years. Some fail for reasons outside executives' control, like global pandemics and economic downturns. However, most labs and incubators fail for reasons that are within executives' control but are blamed on external events. Among those controllable reasons is a single choice, an answer to a question that most executives don't even know they're being asked, which drives every other decision they make:

Are you willing to trade safety for growth?

Most people answer no. Safety is the logical and rational choice. It keeps you employed and your reputation in good standing. It promises minimal interruptions to your success and maximum flexibility if you decide to pursue bigger and better opportunities.

Innovation
is not an idea
problem.
**It is a leadership
problem.**

If you answer yes, people tell you you're nonsensical, irrational, and radical because success isn't guaranteed. You're risking everything—your bonus, your job, your reputation—for the *chance* of growth. And when you choose growth in the context of corporate innovation, you are choosing to do things differently, take risks, and challenge the status quo. You choose these things even though you *know* the odds are against you and that you're more likely to end up as a cautionary tale than an inspiring legend.

There is no wrong answer to the question.

There is only your answer, the one you believe is best for you personally and professionally.

If you choose safety, the innovation you oversee is safe, low risk, and incremental. It keeps the company moving forward, no faster or slower than competitors, and ill prepared for a market or technological disruption. You'll get your bonus, promotion, and peer recognition. Things may get a bit better, but nothing will truly change.

If you choose growth, you'll push boundaries, inspire others, expand how your organization sees itself, catapult it ahead of your competitors, and define a world that doesn't yet exist. Or you'll lose your bonus or your job. There's no middle ground. Because the middle ground is safe. Nothing changes there, and you are all about making change happen.

How to Be the Solution

This book is your guide to becoming the solution your organization needs to do the impossible: innovate within an established and successful organization. It's based on the stories of real-life executives like you who confidently claim the title of innovation leader—someone who creates new things that create value (innovation) and inspires other people to follow (leader).

At the heart of this book is a framework for a holistic approach to innovation. It is based on my experience with companies that transformed themselves into successful innovators because their leaders approached innovation as a system, developing and investing in each part simultaneously.

The ABCs of Innovation may seem simple, but it is the mental and intellectual equivalent of keeping dozens of plates spinning without ever letting one fall. It requires constant attention, nurturing, and evolution to build the momentum necessary to achieve a return on your investment in three years.

Three years leading corporate innovation can feel like a lifetime of throwing yourself against a brick wall. When a small chunk of mortar finally falls out, you celebrate like the whole wall came down. And one day, the wall does fall. I promise.

I've seen it happen. For the past twenty-five years, I've walked in your shoes and alongside others as they walked. As a part of innovation teams and executive boards determining their fates, I understand what both sides need and want, and why what is said and done is frustratingly different. I also know how to knock out pieces of mortar and then whole bricks so you can lead your team and your organization into a future they could only imagine.

A future you saw all along.

Are you ready to start your innovation journey? If you've read this far, I assume the answer is yes. The first stop on our journey is the ABCs of Innovation: what they are and why they're both familiar and different from what you already know.

Ready? Let's go!

2

The ABCs
of Innovation

THE ABCS ARE different from the usual corporate innovation
approach because they require you to actively build (no delegating!)
three very different things in very different ways over the course of
three years. So before you learn about the ABCs and what you'll do,
it's important to know why you need to do so many different things
in different ways for so long.

Three Years of Innovation

To understand why 90 percent of corporate innovation incubators and
labs are shut down within three years,* it's helpful to understand the
pattern that the rise and fall of corporate innovation efforts looks like.

---

* Now, not every executive responsible for innovation leads an incubator or a lab.
There are lots of ways for organizations to structure their innovation efforts. But
if you're hoping that I'm about to tell you that adopting a different structure
buys you more time, I'm sorry to disappoint you.

Year 1

Year 1 is great because everyone is excited. The C-suite is excited because they can point to you, your team, and your budget as evidence that innovation is a strategic priority and that they really are committed to creating the next version of the company. You're excited because you finally have the freedom to create something, change the things that are broken, and chart a new path for yourself, your career, and your organization.

Life is rainbows and unicorns.

Well, except for the quarterly update meetings. At first they're excitement-filled story swaps about all the cool things you and your team are doing and the interesting things you're learning. However, they gradually become less about stories and more about PowerPoint slides, data charts, and questions about ROI and when you'll start producing results. But you're not worried. Innovation takes time, and all those questions about results are from people who just don't get it.

You're making progress and learning a lot. You have results, just not ones that can be measured in dollars and cents (or euros, kroner, pesos, or any other currency).

Year 2

You carried the momentum from last year into this one. Your team is doing great, working together like a dream with just the right amount of tension and debate. People from other parts of the organization are curious about what you're doing and may even ask you to host a lunch-and-learn or a training session for their team.

Life is sunny skies and a gentle breeze.

But those quarterly meetings are getting irritating. Your stakeholders don't care about the customer insights you've unearthed or how you're using them to design disruptive products and radical business models. They don't even care that you shared what you learned with other teams in the organization so they could benefit

90 percent of corporate innovation incubators and labs **are shut down within three years.**

from your fantastic work. All they seem to care about is revenue, ROI, and time to break even.

It doesn't help that there are rumors that a recession will start in six months, core business revenue is coming in below expectations, or supply chain shortages could result in missed shipments. But those aren't your problems. Those are the core business's problems. Problems that innovation will one day overcome and render obsolete.

Year 3

The core business's problems are now your problems. Someone got spooked, and budgets got cut. There's a hiring freeze, and all spending must now get president-level (or higher) approval. Your plans to run a few pilots and maybe even a limited launch this year are on hold as those resources are needed elsewhere, specifically in the core business, where they have a known and guaranteed ROI.

All those people you helped last year are suddenly too busy for the coffee or follow-up chat you scheduled to check in on how they and their teams are getting on with the new tools and templates you shared. Demand for hackathons, shark tanks, and field trips to Silicon Valley evaporate as people hunker down, focusing on their daily tasks and worrying about potential layoffs.

Life is rainstorms with the chance of apocalypse.

As for those quarterly meetings, they still happen, but fewer people attend. You try to schedule one-on-one meetings to follow up with the people who couldn't attend, but they're all too busy. Ultimately, you start canceling meetings because most stakeholders have "sudden and unavoidable schedule conflicts."

At the end of the year, your boss thanks you for all your work, assures you that innovation is still a priority, and then informs you that the organization needs you to be an enabler, not a creator, so your team is reorganized into a center of excellence, focused on training teams that express interest. Your boss also mentions that because innovation is now a cost center and it's unclear how much demand there is for your services, your budget is slashed, and your team is now you and one other person. Your boss reassures you that you'll keep your title and pay, but you'll now report to someone who was previously your peer because your boss is too busy with more important priorities.

The apocalypse arrived.

Innovation went out not with a bang but with a whimper.

But here's a hard fact: you're not the victim, and you could have been the savior.

Most people read this story, shake their heads, and say, "What a shame. If only the poor innovation executive had more time. If only a recession hadn't hit, the largest business line's revenue hadn't dropped, or the supply chain hadn't hiccupped, everything would be okay. The budget wouldn't have been slashed, the head count wouldn't have been cut, and those annoying, short-sighted stakeholders would have asked the right questions at those quarterly meetings."

It's easy to play the victim if this is your story. Most managers do. They point to everything outside their control that causes problems, slows them down, and blocks their progress. They don't see the dozen or more things they could have done to prevent problems or minimize the impact of changes.

The fact is that there is *always* an economic worry on the horizon, a financial metric coming in lower than expected, or an operational hiccup. People *always* ask tough questions, demand quantifiable results, and try to undercut you when you can't produce. There are *always* executives who prioritize short-term decisions and immediate results over long-term growth and a legacy of innovation.

Managers, like the one in the story, use things outside their control as excuses.

Leaders see them as challenges.

Innovation leaders see them as opportunities.

Managers use things outside their control as excuses. Leaders see them as challenges. **Innovation leaders see them as opportunities.**

The ABCs of Innovation and Growth

As a leader, you know you can't spend one fiscal quarter focused only on finance, neglecting everything else, then the next quarter focused on marketing, and so on. You need to keep an eye on everything, monitoring and managing the intersections and leading the whole business, not just pieces and parts. You take a holistic approach to managing your core business. And yet most innovation approaches focus on pieces and parts—devising an innovation structure and process, or developing lots of ideas, or building a culture of innovation.

The ABCs are a holistic approach to innovation, combining all the required elements and helping you design, manage, and evolve them together for lasting success.

They're also not really the ABCs. They are, technically, the BACs because the B, behavior, is the most important element. It's the one that only you can do. Without it, nothing else matters. So I always write about behavior first. Why then do I call them the ABCs? Mostly, it's because ABC is easy to remember—but also it's because BAC makes me think of blood alcohol content. Which is not what we're here to talk about.

B Is for Behavior

Behavior is where successful innovation leaders start. They know that their motivations and aspirations matter as much as the numbers the C-suite expects them to produce. They understand that innovation and operations are entirely different worlds and that what made them successful in one area dooms them in the other. They are aware that everything they say and do is interpreted and analyzed by people across the organization as signs of whether innovation is a strategic imperative or a management flavor of the month.

This is, by far, the most challenging and essential part of the ABCs, because you are the only one who can do the work. Most executives claim they don't have time to do this work. Innovation leaders know that "I don't have time" means "It's not a priority," and there is no greater priority than being the leader that innovation needs. Behavior is the key, which means you're the key.

A Is for Architecture

Architecture is the strategy, structures, processes, governance, metrics, incentives, and all the other left-brained, logical, tangible, business-y stuff that determines how your team works, how decisions get made, and whether or not progress is happening.

It's where most executives start. It's familiar, and they're confident that because they have managed people, processes, structures, metrics, and governance before, they can do it again. They believe it's a safe place to start because it looks and feels like operations, so investments and activities can be easily explained to more senior stakeholders.

It's the wrong place to start. Every organization is perfectly designed to achieve the results it achieves. If you start designing and building before you know what you want to achieve, you're likely to build the wrong thing. Even if the CEO told you to build a $250 million business in three years, other results must be factored into how your team operates. Building a newer or better mousetrap is a bad approach when you're trying to catch a unicorn.

C Is for Culture

Culture is values demonstrated through behavior. You get to create your team's culture but not your organization's. That already exists, and you must work with it, slowly and over time.

Creating, or even recreating, a culture of innovation across an organization is often a lagging indicator that results from a prolonged commitment to and investment in architecture and behavior. It's also terribly fragile. A single executive change often spells doom not just for the team but also for the culture. But there are things you can do to accelerate the creation of a culture of innovation and, ideally, build one that can outlast the leadership, investment, and economic changes that threaten it.

C is also for cookie. You'll need those too. I recommend chocolate chip.

Onward!

This book is your map through the next three years. During your journey, you'll encounter Hope in year 1, Faith in year 2, and Victor in year 3, all corporate innovators* whose stories illustrate the ABCs and prove that it's possible to be in the 10 percent of innovators who succeed.

---

* Hope, Faith, and Victor are all based on real people, and 85 percent of the stories you'll read are true. Their names and those of their companies and colleagues have been changed. Also some details have been added, changed, or removed to better illustrate a point.

Know Your Innovation Leadership Toolkit

INNOVATION IS NOT a spectator sport. But all too often it's treated that way by executives who think they can pop in and out of the process, render judgment, bark orders, and then disappear for a few months.

If you want to be an innovation leader (and I assume you do because you're reading this book), you can't be a spectator. You need to be actively involved in the work, and you need tools so that your work is effective, efficient, fun, and ultimately successful. Luckily, you have easy access to the most essential tools.

Tool #1: TL;DRs and Know Yours

This book is designed to be destroyed—by you when you highlight, dog-ear, and sticky-note it until it's falling apart in your hands. It's designed so that you can return to it again and again to quickly find the advice, tips, tricks, and support you'll need through your journey.

In addition to Hope's, Faith's, and Victor's stories and the chapters that break down the ABCs to explain why each innovator's approach or action is essential and how to do it, you'll find two more things:

1   **TL;DR:** At the end of each ABC chapter is a one-page summary of the key points in the chapter. Think of these TL;DRs as your quick-reference guides that you can easily flip to for a ten-second reminder of what you read in the preceding chapter.

2 **Know Your:** Like the one you're reading right now, the other
   Know Your sections step out of the narrative briefly to provide
   you with foundational and practical information and advice.
   Use each Know Your as a starting point for your work, and share
   them with others to establish a common language for innovation
   and a shared understanding of how you and your team work.

Tool #2: Pen and Paper

Throughout this book, but especially in the earlier chapters, I'll ask
you questions to inform how you design, manage, and evolve your
ABCs of Innovation. Your impulse may be to pause to think about
your answer, highlight or underline the question, jot a note in the
margin, or dog-ear the page.

Instead, I want you to pull out a notebook, tablet, or scrap of
paper and write down the answers. And I do mean "write down"
quite literally. Writing, not typing, is critical at this point, and not
just because I'm old-fashioned and think cursive should still be
taught in schools.

Research conducted by the National Institute of Information
and Communications Technology, Princeton, and other institutions
suggests handwriting is a better tool than typing when thinking
through motivations, self-reflection, and making commitments.
This is because handwriting:

- Demands more cognitive engagement that typing

- Enhances the quality of self-reflection and goal-setting and
  improves mindfulness when done deliberately and intentionally,
  requiring focused attention

- Encourages critical thinking and allows for better memory retention, which is beneficial when making commitments and processing motivations

Write whatever comes to your mind first. Don't think about your answers. Don't worry about forming complete sentences or being grammatically correct. Just write whatever pops into your head.

This process, known as freewriting, taps into your subconscious to generate creative ideas and new perspectives. It creates space for you to explore your thoughts without the intrusion of your inner critic or self-censor. You're also more likely to write honest answers to these questions. Answers that give you the confidence to move forward, guidance as you face decisions, and reassurance when you run into barriers and dilemmas.

Write down your answers so you can return to them when you need to.

And you will need to.

Tool #3: Treats

The references to cookies throughout this book are not accidental. They're inspired by growing evidence of the impact and importance of the gut-brain axis—a two-way communication network between the brain and the gastrointestinal tract—on how we think, act, and feel.

In a nutshell, neurons rely on neurotransmitters, like serotonin and dopamine, to tell our cells what to do. With 100 million neurons in our brains and almost 500 billion neurons in our guts, it's no surprise that neurotransmitters are made in both the brain and gastrointestinal tract, creating a link between the cognitive and emotional centers in our brain. The result is that what we eat impacts both our mood and our cognitive abilities.

The key to maximizing our cognitive abilities and improving our moods is glucose. Glucose is the brain's primary source of fuel, and carbohydrates are our primary source of glucose. When our brains run low on glucose because we're not eating enough carbs, our serotonin spikes, making us feel fatigued, and our dopamine plummets, decreasing focus and motivation.

It's not only carbs that we need. Other foods that increase good bacteria in our gut—like dark chocolate, red wine, almonds, blueberries, and some cheeses—also boost our mood and cognitive abilities. So, if you want to be as smart and positive as possible, be sure to have easy access to treats while you work.

YEAR ONE

3

Hope

THE CEO looked across his desk at Hope and sighed. "When it comes to innovation, I feel like I'm sitting at a poker table, placing bets, and all the lights are off."

Hope smiled, pulled her white paper out of her briefcase, and slid it across the desk.

Three Months Earlier

MaXperience (MX) was widely recognized as one of the world's most innovative companies, a reputation in which its CEO took great pride.

Hope disagreed.

She heard talk about disruption and business model innovation, but she didn't see any action. What she did see was the same thing she always saw: small efficiency gains in manufacturing, tiny improvements in product performance, and dazzling new aesthetic designs. In executive meetings, Hope struggled to control her eye rolls every time someone presented a new thread color as "a radical breakthrough destined to redefine the industry." The gap between perception and reality infuriated her, but she also knew that such gaps signal new opportunities. She needed to figure out how to grasp it.

When it comes
to innovation,
I feel like I'm sitting
at a poker table,
**placing bets,
and all the lights
are off.**

She already had a good track record. Five years ago, she saw a similar gap in MX's supply chain and transformed it from a liability to the industry's leader. In the process, she earned herself a promotion to vice president and a reputation as a change agent—and occasional troublemaker.

But the last opportunity was obvious: it was triggered by a PR crisis, consumer boycotts, and government regulations. This opportunity was obvious only to Hope. Everyone else was proud of the status quo and keen to maintain it. Hope knew she needed to tread lightly.

She started writing a white paper.

It began as a tool to gather and organize her thoughts, but it evolved into a means to communicate her vision: a team dedicated to resolving the innovator's dilemma by working on "moonshots" that supported long-term aspirations but didn't fit cleanly into existing businesses.

Like her supply chain team, this innovation team would be structurally separate but strategically linked to the core business to ensure that innovations continued to be supported and nurtured once they left the incubator and were integrated into existing business units. Her role as its leader would also, she hoped, catapult her to chief innovation officer—or even CEO.

Now, all she had to do was wait for the right moment to share her white paper. And when the CEO expressed his frustration with innovation investments, she seized it.

Month 1: Lay the Foundation

The CEO read her white paper and said he fully embraced her vision. Except for two things: her proposed team couldn't initiate new projects because, as a new centralized team with a cross-company mandate, it would be seen as a threat to existing innovation teams, and she wouldn't be promoted to chief innovation officer as she hoped. Instead, Peter, a well-known and respected executive, would be named president and Hope would be his second-in-command.

Hope was furious. The CEO *said* he endorsed her idea, but he completely changed the purpose of the team and her role in it. After a couple of days simmering on the unfairness of the CEO's corporate doublespeak, she became focused. She saw that the CEO-endorsed path could still accomplish her original goals.

She assembled a team, pulling a handful of her most trusted people out of their day jobs, and supported them with a small team of consultants who had experience establishing innovation teams and helping companies avoid disruption. As the team settled into their chairs, Hope began to tell the story of the team: how her vision of it began when she saw the limits of the company's innovation efforts, that the vision sparked to life when the CEO expressed frustration, and that by gathering some of the most creative and trusted people with whom she had worked, that spark was becoming a flame. When she saw people leaning forward in their chairs, eager to be part of the story, she revealed their mission: "turn the lights on" by compiling MX's first-ever enterprise-wide innovation portfolio, and "keep the lights on" by creating a structure and process to continually monitor and manage the portfolio and recommend changes to ensure it would deliver on MX's strategies and vision.

Hope's handpicked team all had years of experience within the company. They knew what worked and what didn't. They also had strong relationships with key managers across the organization—or they thought they did.

After a few early conversations, Hope and her team realized that before they could "turn the lights on" for the CEO, they needed to convince others in the organization that the lights *should* be turned on and that everyone needed to be involved in making it happen. It wouldn't be easy.

For starters, "innovation" meant different things to different people. To people working on products, it meant everything from minor improvements to major new product lines. To people working in other functions, it meant process optimization, integration of new IT, radically new manufacturing systems, and even new-to-the-world inventions. In a company that prided itself on being innovative, "innovation" meant whatever a manager needed it to mean to get the funding and resources required.

Hope and her team realized that if "innovation" could mean anything, it meant absolutely nothing. To compile the portfolio, they needed it to mean something. They needed a definition. One that was broad enough to include everything already labeled "innovation" (because removing that label from a project would go as well as taking an ice cream cone from a kid) and specific enough to meaningfully differentiate projects based on their investment levels, anticipated time to market, estimated financial contribution, and overall impact.

They chose to start with the classic terminology of core, adjacent, and radical, defining each type of innovation based on how it would create value (existing or new customers and existing or new offerings) and how it would capture and deliver value (revenue versus cost, existing capabilities or new). Before sharing the definitions with others, the team applied them to Hope's supply chain team's portfolio.

It didn't work.

Despite their in-depth understanding of each project, the team couldn't agree on how to categorize each one. Most projects seemed to fit multiple definitions, and it was easy to game the system by applying the definition that would lead to the desired portfolio split.

The team tried again, keeping the terms core, adjacent, and radical and adjusting the definitions. After days of experimenting, the team developed definitions that were both broad and differentiating and could be applied with minimal debate.

Definitions, unfortunately, don't turn on the lights. The CEO didn't only want to know what he was investing in. He needed to know what to expect from his investments. Definitions addressed the former but not the latter. Executives, however, were hesitant to share plans or forecasts because they didn't want to commit to results from projects that could change or be canceled.

To manage the tension between the CEO's needs and executives' fears, the team developed a framework to track both the progress of the projects' development and the team's confidence in their projections by evaluating the degree to which reliable and robust data supported critical assumptions. As unorthodox as using confidence rather than activities to assess a project's status was, the team discovered that by identifying critical assumptions for each project and evaluating the reliability and robustness of the data used to validate the assumptions, they could consistently track, assess, and make decisions about every type of innovation.

People turn on lights... if they want to. With the foundational elements of a shared language and framework in place, the team now had to convince others to join them in turning on the lights—a challenging task in a decentralized organization with a culture that values autonomy and the spirit of entrepreneurship. Hope and her team needed a call to action that would resonate throughout the organization and feel deeply personal to the executives and managers they needed to enroll. Knowing that a significant portion of executives' compensation was tied to stock performance, which was, in turn, directly impacted by the company's ability to deliver on expectations, the team posed a simple question: "To deliver our five-year revenue goal, how much new revenue needs to come from things that don't yet exist?"

And then they revealed the answer: "We need to create the equivalent of two Facebooks in the next five years."

Everyone was suddenly eager to help.

Month 2: Work with Other Innovation Teams

Finally, it was time to compile the portfolio, but the team knew it wouldn't be as straightforward as sending an email request and analyzing the data sent back. Gathering data about innovation activities and investments across the company required careful management of the company's secretive (even within the company) culture. Knowing that innovation teams would perceive any request for information as a threat, Hope used her positional authority to invite executives in charge of each product business unit (BU) to participate in a series of working sessions to discuss their resource needs, IP requirements, and open innovation efforts.

The first workshop was a make-or-break moment for Hope's team—either they would get the data to compile a company-wide portfolio of innovation projects and investments, or they would alienate their colleagues, creating an obstacle impossible to overcome.

Hope believed deeply in the importance of an empowered team, so once the team was up and running, she often slid into the background, supporting and advising them as needed. But this meeting was too important, and the attendees' reactions were too uncertain. She needed to establish the team's importance and credibility, and that couldn't be done by proxy or from the back of the room.

Seated at the head of the table, her back to a plate glass window through which the sun beamed in, blinding the attendees, Hope kicked off the meeting. She thanked everyone for coming and outlined the context and goals for the session. Once the expectations for the session were clear, she turned to the BU innovation leader seated to her left and asked him to share his portfolio. He ticked down a list of projects, interrupted only by clarifying questions about the type of innovation and its place in the development framework, and reassurances that this was simply a "documentation exercise" and nothing was being judged or evaluated.

It could have progressed like this for hours, with attendees wondering why this was a workshop, not an email. But half an hour in, everything changed when a project elicited an unexpected "Hey, we're working on that too." Over the three hours, dozens of projects were revealed as being worked on by two or more teams. The chatter in the room grew louder as BU leads shared project details and discussed ways to pool resources and work together. No one noticed that once it was clear that the BU innovation leads were engaged and cooperative, Hope had quietly slipped out of the room.

It was early evening when the last person left the conference room, and the team could declare victory. They had the info they needed, and every BU lead had several projects they could accelerate through collaboration with another team.

Having experienced a personal benefit from the first workshop, the BU leads eagerly participated in the following two workshops—sharing their IP developments and needs and outlining their existing and planned joint ventures and partnerships.

Month 3: Turn the Lights On

With the data from the first workshop, Hope's team started crunching the portfolio numbers. The results were not what anyone expected.

The CEO expected a 50/25/25 split across core, adjacent, and radical innovation. The team's analysis revealed an 85/10/5 split. That wasn't the only surprise. The data also indicated that most projects were concentrated at the very beginning of the process or the very end, and the ones at the beginning had, in many cases, been there for years. Not a promising sign for a company that needed to create billions of dollars of net new revenue in only five years.

The lights were on, and it wasn't pretty.

The lights were on, **and it wasn't pretty.**

In the ugliness, Hope saw the opportunity to move closer to her goal of leading a moonshot team.

As her team prepared the innovation portfolio for the CEO, she prepared a plan. To shift the portfolio closer to the expected 50/25/25 split by the end of the year, her team would:

1 produce quarterly updates, highlighting portfolio shifts and risks;

2 act as an accelerator by providing physical space and hands-on support to BU teams working on radical innovation; and

3 incubate moonshots that didn't rise to the top of BUs' strategic or operational priorities but did align with MX's strategies and vision.

When she shared the portfolio and her "rapid rebalancing plan" with her boss, Peter, he embraced it. Except for one thing. He informed Hope that, after several discussions with the CEO, her team was unlikely to expand in the coming months and that some current team members had to return to their previous roles. She needed to do more with less by keeping the remaining members of her innovation team focused on monitoring and updating the portfolio.

Hope was frustrated. There was that corporate doublespeak again.

She was also focused. The path to her ultimate goal of running a moonshot team still existed. It just had more bends than she expected.

Three months later, the team presented an updated portfolio. Nothing had changed, despite the CEO's request that BU innovation teams "clean up" their portfolios by killing stalled projects and starting new projects that were either adjacent or radical. It was finally clear to the CEO and the president that they would not get the new results they wanted by pursuing innovation the way they always had.

At the end of the first year, Hope was on the brink of achieving her goal. Thanks to the relationships that her team had developed with the BUs as a result of their portfolio monitoring efforts, BU leaders frequently asked Hope's team for advice, perspective, and support, resulting in a doubling of investment in radical innovation. Even more exciting was that BUs started asking Hope's team to work on ideas the BU developed but couldn't pursue because they didn't obviously advance short-term priorities or they required collaboration with other BUs.

As planning for year 2 began, Hope was confident that her moonshot accelerator was about to become a reality.

4

Behavior
Instincts, Identity, and Choices

GEORGE COSTANZA could be the patron saint of corporate innovators.

In the classic *Seinfeld* episode "The Opposite," George, Jerry, and Elaine sit together in the diner. As usual, George's life is a disaster. He's just lost another job, been dumped by another girlfriend, and moved back in with his parents. As he laments the decisions that brought him to this point, Jerry makes a wry observation: "If every instinct you have is wrong, then the opposite would have to be right."

With nothing to lose, George embraces the suggestion. He immediately walks up to a beautiful woman at the nearby lunch counter. "My name is George. I'm unemployed, and I live with my parents." By the end of the episode, George has a hot new girlfriend, his own apartment, and his dream job with the New York Yankees.

Be George Costanza (but only the George from this episode).

All the instincts, knowledge, and experiences that made you successful in operating roles lead you astray in innovation—because innovation is the opposite of operations.

In an operating role, you are an expert because you know more than you don't know. You have the knowledge and experience required to predict outcomes, evaluate proposals, and ask pointed questions designed to get the team to the next major milestones. It's what Columbia Business School professor Rita McGrath calls a high-knowledge, low-assumption environment.

Innovation is the opposite. It's a low-knowledge, high-assumption environment in which you are anything but an expert. You *don't know* more than you *do* know, so success requires asking questions, learning quickly, making decisions based on heuristics and best practices, and responding rapidly to surprises.

Leading innovation requires you to take the opposite of the approach that earned you great success up to this point. In the words of Marshall Goldsmith, "What got you here won't get you there." In the spirit of George Costanza, do the opposite.

Your Innovation Instincts

Who are you?

It's such a simple question. Whenever we're asked who we are or to "tell us a bit about yourself," we usually rattle off a list of personal roles like daughter, husband, friend, or professional titles like VP of this or manager of that. We may talk about where we live, where we grew up, or what we do in our free time.

George was single, unemployed, and living with his parents. Hope was an innovator, change agent, and troublemaker. You may aspire to be an innovator, an inspiration, or even an icon. You can achieve those aspirations in this role. But first you must know who you are and what makes you amazing today. So get out your pen and paper.

Who Are You Right Now?

This is your foundation, the place from which you build every-thing else—your role, your team, your strategy, and all your accomplishments.

Write down all the roles you play. You can restrict the list to just your professional roles, or if you're really courageous, you can expand it to include your personal ones too. Remember to put "role model" and "innovation leader" on this list because, like it or not, you're both things now.

You're a role model, not because you have a fancy title or because you are intelligent, good-looking, incredibly talented, or any number of other wonderful things (even though you are also those wonderful things). You're a role model because people in your organization look to you for clues about what they should believe, how they should behave, and what they need to do to be successful.

As an innovation leader, you set the standard for how innovation is perceived, prioritized, discussed, pursued, and communicated in your organization. Everything you say and do is scrutinized as people, skeptical of past innovation efforts, try to discern whether innovation is a strategic priority or a public relations gambit.

Hope was the innovator, change agent, and troublemaker every-one knew her to be. She was also a single mother, a former DJ, an aspiring artist, and an activist for environmental causes. She knew that while she inspired loyalty and admiration from some colleagues, others viewed her as ruthless, untrustworthy, and selfish.

What Makes You, You?

Once you list who you are, list all the things you do that make you awesome. Don't be humble. You are great at what you do and must keep doing some of those things. You must also stop doing some of them, but we'll get to that in a moment. Most executives list qualities like decisiveness, action orientation, ability to consistently deliver results, technical expertise, and communication as drivers of their success. Go deeper. Write down stories of times when you've been great. What was the context? Was it high knowledge or high assumption? What did you do? Why did you do it? What made it the right choice in that context?

Hope could see the potential of every situation and every person. It's what enabled her to see opportunities for innovation months, even years, before others did. It also meant she could see that people and situations weren't living up to their potential, resulting in a daily mood that fluctuated between annoyed and enraged. Hope was also fearless, relentless, and resilient. She wasn't afraid to upset people, but she was very skilled at working the system—knowing who to talk to and how in order to build support for her cause.

What you've written down is who you are today. It's what makes you great at what you do. You don't need to change who you are or stop doing these things. What you do need to do, however, is recognize that these are your instincts and that they may not be right in every circumstance. In some circumstances, like innovation, you need to do the opposite.

What Might the Opposite Look Like?

This next step requires a bit of imagination and creativity because it asks you to think about how the qualities and behaviors that make you great today could lead to disaster in a different context and how you might need to adapt, amplify, or even forget these mindsets, behaviors, and habits to succeed in the context of innovation.

For example:

- **Decisiveness:** Ideas are a dime a dozen, and decisions are gold. How do you make decisions? Do you need years of data, dozens of external benchmarks, and reams of evidence? If you do, you'll need to do the opposite in innovation because there is no data for things that have never been done before.

Recognize
your instincts
because in some
circumstances,
**you might need to
do the opposite.**

- **Action orientation:** If decisions are gold, action is priceless. How many approvals or pledges of support do you need before you act? Do you need everyone in agreement and cheering you on before you take your first step? If you wait to act until you're certain you've made the right choice and everyone approves, you won't act at all in innovation.

- **Technical expertise:** You know a lot about a lot of things. What do you do when confronted with something you don't know about? Do you ignore it, procrastinate, delegate, start researching, or dive in and hope you figure it out? When you're innovating, you are doing something new, and while your technical expertise may help with some things, it may also close your mind to new ways of thinking about or doing things.

- **Communication:** When and how do you communicate? Do you wait until you know everything and have a plan? Do you wait until you have the results? Or do you communicate regularly, sharing updates even when the outcome is uncertain or the outcome isn't what you wanted?

Hope knew she didn't have a sterling reputation and that challenging a core element of MaXperience's identity could leave her ostracized and powerless despite her supply chain success. That's why she chose to write a white paper and be patient. She knew a well-reasoned and data-based approach would more likely be listened to over an emotional plea and anecdotal evidence. It's also why she chose to wait for the CEO to express frustration about innovation, instead of trying to convince him to be frustrated by the current state.

Now that you have your list of opposites, identify the qualities and behaviors that need to change and why. For example, you may need to make decisions more slowly and communicate more regularly. Other behaviors, like your ability to build strong relationships, may not need to change. You'll also notice things on the list that are, as one of my clients likes to say, "contextual." You may need to do the opposite, or you may need to do what you usually do. The right answer depends on the context. Note which bucket—change, keep, it's contextual—each quality and behavior fall into, because it's time to make choices.

Your Organization's Identity

You're not the only one with instincts.

Your organization has instincts too.

Just as the next three years will challenge you to do the opposite of your instincts, you will challenge the organization to do the opposite of its instincts.

But first you need to know what its instincts are. Keep your pen ready as you read.

Who Are We?

Talking about an organization's culture, strategies, structures, processes, policies, or even people is not unusual. What is unusual to discuss is its identity. But every organization has one, and it affects their strategy, structure, processes, policies, and people.

An organization's identity is "a shared belief amongst organization members about 'who we are.'" It often emerges over time and can change as the mission, operations, and external environment evolve. However, change is slow and difficult, and organizations often resist it because a shared understanding of who we are requires "a shared understanding of what activities constitute appropriate action. Put differently, 'who we are' has implications for 'what we should do.'"

Who are we? What should we do? The answers define the core of your organization's identity.

Write down your answers to these two questions. Then ask other people in the organization how they would answer the questions. Talk to people above and below you. Talk to your peers in different functions and geographies. Whatever you do, don't read the website or the annual report. The answers you find there are manufactured statements specifically designed to look good and sound better. The answers you and your colleagues provide, based on everyday experiences, are the real answers.

For Hope's company, the answers were simple: they made technically advanced products and sold them to consumers through retailers. The company was inspiring, edgy, and elite, a place people aspired to work and were impressed by when they saw it on résumés. That's why Hope's focus on business models that didn't involve retail and instead were moonshots that focused on services met resistance. She challenged the company's identity.

Hope's not alone. Most innovation leaders quickly encounter tension between their organization's desire to do things differently and the invisible but overwhelming need to preserve the organization as it is by continuing to do what it always does. This leads us to the next question.

What Are We Willing to Do?

With all due respect to the academics quoted above, "What should we do?" is the wrong question. The right question is "What *will* we do?" Most organizations know what they *should* do. It is why they create innovation teams and acquire companies in new industries or geographies. But "should do" and "will do" are entirely different things, as evidenced by the fact that the teams and acquisitions rarely achieve their desired results.

Unlike the previous questions that required essay-level answers, this one is multiple choice.

Option 1: Identity-Enhancing. Most innovations, even disruptive ones like the disk drives that Clayton Christensen studied, are identity-enhancing in that they strengthen and reinforce how the organization sees itself and defines its core capabilities and activities. Identity-enhancing innovations respect the preexisting boundaries of industry and market definitions, even if they seem like radical departures from a company's traditional business.

For example, Warby Parker launched in 2010 as an online-only eyeglass retailer. To overcome consumer hesitancy to buy eyeglasses without trying them on first, the company offered a home try-on program: consumers could select up to five frames to try on at home for free for five days before making their selection and sending the frames back. Over the following decade-plus, Warby Parker expanded to 227 stores, developed its own point-of-sale system in 2015, and built a 34,000-square-foot optical lab in 2017 to reduce and ultimately eliminate reliance on third-party manufacturers. These activities contradict Warby Parker's original low-cost, online-only business model. But they are consistent and even enhance and advance the company's identity as a provider of fashionable, reasonably priced corrective eyewear.

Option 2: Identity-Stretching. Identity-stretching innovations are more challenging because they broaden and shift an organization's identity. These innovations become essential when an organization faces a continuously shifting landscape of customer behaviors or preferences, sources of competitive advantage, regulations, technology, geopolitical alignment, or economic conditions.

Alessi, an Italian kitchen utensil company, used identity-stretching innovations to transform itself from a manufacturer of cold-pressed steel serving tools like trays, baskets, and teapots into an internationally renowned producer of high-end household products, so famous for its design and aesthetics that its products are exhibited in art museums around the world. When Alberto Alessi, the founder's grandson, joined the organization in 1970, the company was the technological leader in industrial-scale production of functional steel products for home use. He saw an opportunity to be more than that and invited sculptors like Giò Pomodoro and Salvador Dalí to design small works of functional art to be produced on an industrial scale. This small experiment triggered decades of design, manufacturing, and distribution innovation. It also saved Alessi from the "race to the bottom" fate of most low-cost and low-profit manufacturers by evolving its identity from "industrial producer" to "artistic mediator" to "crafts workshop" to "dream factory" with consistent growth year over year.

Option 3: Identity-Challenging. Hope's plan, however, went beyond identity-enhancing and identity-stretching to focus on identity-challenging innovations that "can pose major problems for organizations." (This is the understatement of the year.) When faced with innovations, or even the specter of innovations, that challenge an organization's notion of who it is and what it does, research shows that executives tend to do one of three things: they ignore the innovation opportunity; they acknowledge it but don't pursue it; or they notice it, attempt to pursue it, "in some cases failing to innovate, while in others implementing approaches for realigning the innovation and identity."

Kodak is a classic example of an organization pursuing option 3 and failing. It recognized the innovative opportunity created by digital technology but framed it to fit its existing identity as a film company serving the world's best photographers. Hope is the rare example of someone who pursued option 3 and succeeded. But note that she first had to overcome options 1 and 2 by earning trust and credibility with her key stakeholders and delivering the results that mattered most to them before she had permission to pursue the identity-challenging moonshots she believed to be vital to the company's future.

People
want change,
**but they
don't want to
be changed.**

Determining what your organization is willing to do, specifically how open it is to having its identity challenged, is not easy. If you do what you did with the previous questions and ask people directly, most claim they're willing to do all these types of innovation. You'll then spend the next two years running into brick walls until you realize that your colleagues are only willing to do new things if it doesn't cost them anything, represent any risk, create any discomfort, or require them to change in any way. People want change, but they don't want to be changed.

Instead, help your stakeholders help you. Our brains are hardwired for tangible examples; the danger of a tiger is hard to understand if you've never seen a tiger, but you immediately understand the threat they pose when you face one. Give your stakeholders examples of innovations you're working on (or would like to work on) that are identity-enhancing, -stretching, or -challenging, and ask for their reactions. Believe the answers they give you because those answers are their instincts. As in Hope's situation, the answers may not be what you want, but they tell you what you have the freedom to do. You may need to help them do the opposite, like George.

Your Innovation Choice

You've learned a lot in the last few pages.

Now it's time to make choices. Get out your pen and paper again.

Your answers to the following two questions are the foundation of everything you are about to create. They influence how you behave as a leader and a role model. Executives who don't make these choices and keep doing what they've always done don't survive the first three years because they never built a solid foundation for innovation. Everything you build—your strategy, your team, your portfolio—are subject to constant shifts in the external environment and internal whims that could lead to their collapse.

Who Do You Choose to Be?

You know who you are today and what the opposite could look like. Now you get to choose who you are as an innovation leader.

Hope didn't change her identity one bit. She was thrilled with her reputation as a visionary who constantly questioned the status quo. Another leader you'll meet in year 2 adjusted her identity when she moved from being a startup founder to an innovation leader in a Global 100 company. She discovered that she needed to do the opposite of her entrepreneurial instincts and slow down, communicate more, and focus as much on relationships as results. The leader you'll meet in year 3 managed to sustain two identities: one focused on learning, experimentation, and breaking the rules when he was with his innovation teams; the other focused on managing processes, minimizing risk, and maximizing returns when he was in an operating role.

If you feel overwhelmed by all of this, that's okay. It's not something we usually do in our day-to-day work. Just remember that whatever you write down is correct because it's what you know right now. It can and will change. What matters is that you know who you are and want to be, as your organization's innovation leader.

What Will You and Won't You Do?

It doesn't matter if you were handed a mandate, strategy, or goal when you accepted responsibility for innovation. It doesn't matter if you were told to build an innovation team, portfolio, or culture. It doesn't even matter if you were given a vague mandate to make the organization more innovative.

What you learned about the organization's identity, the activities that reinforce it, and the limits of its willingness to innovate matters. Now you get to choose what you will and won't do to innovate.

Defining what you will and won't do is essential to setting yourself and your organization up for success. It outlines the results your organization can expect and keeps you and your team focused on the work you love. It's also a helpful way to set expectations, justify what you're working on and why, and quiet others' fears and suspicions that you're trying to meddle in or take over their work.

Think back to Hope's story. She wanted to lead an incubator that challenged her company's identity and created offerings that would disrupt, maybe even destroy, her current company. She was willing to start by creating a portfolio because it could lead to her moonshots. She wasn't willing to work on identity-enhancing innovations, which the company already did well—designing and manufacturing products sold through retailers.

Once you answer the question of what you will and won't work on in innovation, share it with your key stakeholders. Explain what you learned that led you to these choices and why they create value for your organization by advancing its key strategies and priorities. Keep talking, listening, and debating until you agree. Any work done before you reach an agreement is wasted because you either won't want to do it or at least one stakeholder thinks it doesn't need to be done.

You're not holding innovation hostage by refusing to work before everyone agrees on scope. You're efficiently using your scarce resources and providing incentives to progress rapidly. (Corporate doublespeak isn't all bad.)

Once you make your choices, take a breath, have a cookie (still recommending chocolate chip), and get excited. You're about to start building.

TL;DR* Year 1 Behavior

Be George Costanza. Do the opposite of your instincts.

Resist the urge to do what you've always done.

- Write down the qualities, mindsets, and behaviors that make you a great operator. What could the opposite look like?

- Discover your organization's identity by asking people, "Who are we? What do we do?"

- Test your organization's willingness to enhance, stretch, and challenge its identity by offering examples of innovation and gauging people's reactions.

Reflect and decide who you want to be and what you want to do because the choices you make here are the foundation for everything that comes next.

- Who do you choose to be as a leader? What instincts will you follow? What will you ignore?

- What is your definition of innovation? What will it deliver for the organization?

- What do you choose to work on within that definition? Where is the intersection between work you love to do and work your organization values?

---

* TL;DR is internet slang for "too long; didn't read." Of course, you read the chapter (good for you!), but let's be honest, it's easy to forget key points in the hubbub of daily work and leadership. So, to make it easier for you to find and use the tips that enable you to turn bold ideas into tangible results, TL;DR sections are included at the end of each chapter.

Know Your Innovation Types

AS HOPE DID, start by defining "innovation" with your key stakeholders, who control your fate and budget. This may seem like a simple and overly academic place to start. Still, if you don't start here, you'll quickly (and painfully) discover that definitions and expectations diverge, often in ways from which you can't recover.

A few years ago, the CEO of an ed-tech company tasked one of his reports with developing an "innovation mandate" for the organization. We interviewed every member of the executive committee, asking them, among other things, to define innovation. From eight interviews, we collected six different definitions:

- Invention, something new to the world

- Commercially successful invention

- Ideas put into action that create revenue

- New product (of company, industry, or the world)

- New product that creates revenue *or* a new process that decreases cost

- Commercial success from either new capabilities or products

There are common themes—new, revenue, and products—but the potential for misunderstanding and missed expectations is *huge*. In this case, the CEO believed that innovation was an "idea put into action that creates revenue," the CTO thought it was something new to the world, and the executive charged with creating the innovation mandate planned to build a team to support other teams' pursuit of new products or processes. Needless to say, the conversation was far from an academic exercise. It was a necessary strategic discussion that saved time and energy, avoided frustration, and increased the odds of success.

It can *become* an academic conversation if you dwell on it too long.

Definitions change (look at "literally," which now also means "figuratively"). So don't obsess over your decision to the point of analysis paralysis.

Define Innovation

I recommend defining innovation as "something new that creates value" and saving the team's time and energy for defining different types of innovation (which we'll get to in a moment).

The recommended definition is broad by design. In most organizations, innovation is like the cool kids' table in junior high—everyone wants to sit there, but very few people are invited. That kind of exclusivity feels great when you're in the club, but it leads to jealousy, resentment, and even sabotage when you're on the outside. You're not in junior high anymore. Do better.

- **Something** can be any number of things—product, service, process, business model, revenue model, profit model, or distribution channel.

- **New** can mean new to the world (invention), new to your industry or company, or new to your function.

- **Value** includes financial metrics like revenue, cost, and ROI. It also encompasses any metric used to evaluate your company's performance—profit, shareholder return, market share, employee satisfaction, or Net Promoter Score.

Even though it's broad, it does rule things out. Something different but not new isn't innovation. This rules out continuous improvement, optimization, and efficiency efforts to make existing things better, faster, or cheaper. It also rules out efforts that don't create value, like discoveries and inventions that don't (yet) have a known application.

Define at Least Three Different Types of Innovation

Innovation isn't chocolate: you can't spread it all over everything and expect deliciousness. Just as you need different types of chocolate for different types of cookies, you need different types of innovation to drive different types of growth.

Hope and her team chose to break innovation into three types—core, adjacent, and radical—but there are many others you can choose from:

- **Core innovation** improves existing products for existing customers. This type of innovation is also referred to as "incremental" because it involves making small changes or as "sustaining" because its intent is to sustain the business over the next one to three years.

- **Adjacent innovations** introduce new offerings to existing customers or increase the sales of existing solutions to new customers. Swiffer is an example of an adjacent innovation because it was a new product (durable stick with a disposable cleaning cloth) for P&G's existing customers (retailers) and consumers (people who clean their floors).

- **Radical innovations** often have their roots in invention and introduce new solutions to new and existing customers, often using new business models.

- **Disruptive innovation** is a term coined by Harvard professor Clayton Christensen to describe "a process by which a product or service takes root initially in simple applications at the bottom of a market ... and then relentlessly moves upmarket, eventually displacing established competitors." Essentially, disruptive innovations offer poorer performance than other competitors on the market, but because they are offered at a lower price, they are attractive to non-consumers because something is better than nothing. Over time, as the disruptive product's performance improves and existing products add more features to justify increased prices, consumers start switching to the lower-cost "good enough" options.

- **Business model innovation** changes how a company captures and/or delivers value. This could be through the use of new revenue or profit models, different production or delivery processes, or changes to any other part of the company's business model canvas.

There are many other types of innovation, so don't obsess over finding the perfect three (or four) types of innovation for your team. Like Hope's team did, find a few types that people like the sound of and then tweak the definitions to make them work for you and your goals.

5

Architecture
Where, Who, and How

"Would you tell me, please, which way I ought to go from here?"
"That depends a good deal on where you want to get to," said the Cat.
"I don't much care where—" said Alice.
"Then it doesn't much matter which way you go," said the Cat.
LEWIS CARROLL, *Alice's Adventures in Wonderland*

IT'S HARD to argue with that logic. Though I'd add that Alice would be well served to care about where she's going, who she's traveling with, and how she'll get there.

Where Are You Going?

If there's one thing I learned at Harvard Business School, it's that strategy requires making choices. An innovation strategy makes your life easier because it specifies the problems you'll solve. It explains to your stakeholders what you're doing, why, and what's in it for them. It guides who is on your team and how the work gets done.

In the last chapter, you made a lot of choices—who you want to be as an innovation leader, how your behavior brings that to life, and what you will and won't work on. It's tempting to think that all those choices weave together into a strategy.

They don't.

They *inform* your strategy.

In his book *Good Strategy/Bad Strategy*, UCLA Anderson School of Management professor Richard P. Rumelt distinguishes good strategies from bad strategies. Good strategies:

- Are simple and obvious

- State the problem to be solved

- Leverage relative strengths to solve the problem

- Focus efforts by deciding what the organization will and won't do

- Detail actions that reinforce and support each other

Bad strategies:

- Are fluffy buzzword Bingo cards filled with industry jargon and smart-sounding phrases

- Are to-do lists of initiatives people are working on or want to work on

- Obscure the problem or describe it in vague terms

- Focus on blue-sky objectives, goals, and desires rather than decisions and actions

- Fail to acknowledge critical issues or offer impractical solutions

The problem at the heart of your strategy may be simple and obvious, but finding it rarely is. Here's a list of the most common innovation strategies:

- Grow our business.

- Stop losing our customers and employees to more innovative competitors.

- Get good PR so analysts and investors think we're innovative.

Yes, the above items are problems. No, they're not strategies. The problems at the heart of good strategy are the root causes of symptoms like slow growth, lost customers and employees, and declining stock prices. The problems are concrete, not vague, and action-oriented without being lists of tasks. Finding and defining the problems that lead to good strategy takes time, curiosity, and creativity.

The CEO of Hope's company said his problem was the lack of visibility into the innovation portfolio. His real problem was that he wasn't getting the ROI he needed from his innovation investments. Solving *that* problem required more than compiling an innovation portfolio. It required executives to know what ROI the CEO expected, the state of and expectations for the current portfolio, and a plan to shift, manage, and fill a portfolio that would deliver the CEO's growth and ROI expectations. When Hope realized all this, she saw a path to where she wanted to go, starting with a portfolio and ending with moonshots.

"Improve our ROI on innovation as a means to drive growth" is not a strategy. It's closer than "turn the lights on by compiling an innovation portfolio," but it's still vague and fails to acknowledge critical issues. To be a strategy, it needs to be concrete, and nothing is more concrete than money. If your innovation strategy doesn't include a concrete financial definition of success, you won't get all the resources you need, and you definitely won't hold on to them for long. It's time to stop pretending that innovation is just a happy, feel-good, rainbows, unicorns, and pixie dust endeavor and be honest: it's about the money. Nonprofits need grants and donations to deliver their services. Governments levy taxes and fines to fund programs and services. For-profit companies, well, you know the rest. Include it in your strategy.

This is why the growth gap was critical to Hope's success. By calculating the difference between her company's long-term financial goal and what it was projected to deliver based on current plans, she showed that the company needed $15 billion in five years from things that didn't exist, even on paper.

"Generate $15 billion in net new revenue in five years from the design, development, and launch of new to the industry products and services." That's a strategy that tells you where you're going.

Who Are You Going With?

Your team is the most critical architecture decision you make in year 1. I have seen teams bursting at the seams with "high potential" employees fail to make it through the first year because they're overwhelmed by ambiguity and uncertainty despite brilliant strategies and clear goals. I have worked with teams of "misfits," employees who don't fit the existing system or culture, that generated revenue in their first year guided by only the faintest whiff of direction.

Your strategy informs who you need on your team.

Your team determines whether or not your strategy is a success.

You know an organization's priorities by how it allocates its resources. If your organization won't allocate resources full-time to your team, it's a sign that innovation is not a priority; it's a hobby. And don't accept compromises like dotted line reporting and "20 percent time." Dotted lines force people to pick sides because they can't serve both equally well. The originator of 20 percent time, 3M, reduced it to 15 percent, and Google has basically eliminated it. When the originators back away from an idea, follow their lead.

Your strategy informs who you need on your team. **Your team determines whether or not your strategy is a success.**

Innovation leaders rarely inherit a fully staffed team or have the freedom and resources to create their own ideal team. You're more likely to be handed some combination of employees and open job descriptions and told to make it work. And you will, because research indicates that "it is not the selection of people that determines the degree of exploration, but what they are asked to do." When you defined your innovation strategy, including the concrete goal, you did the most impactful thing possible to set your team up for success.

When Hope formed her team, she didn't have a strategy or a concrete goal. She had the next best thing: a team of people with a shared work history. Research shows that "teams that have previously worked together are superior to newly assembled teams" because the team can skip the early awkward stages of learning how to work together and immediately jump into creative exploration and collaborative problem-solving activities.

You'll have a strategy, or the beginnings of one, when you start forming your team. Start small with your team, at least two people plus you. Bigger teams invite scrutiny and set expectations for speed and results you can't deliver. To quote Faith, whom you'll meet in year 2, "Just because one woman can make a baby in nine months doesn't mean nine women can make a baby in one month."

As you select people for your team or consider the people you've been assigned, try to assemble a creative and diverse team. Creativity requires outsiders who don't think the way the organization thinks and insiders who understand why the organization thinks the way it does. Creativity is also fueled by experts who know their field so well that they "push its boundaries with any nontrivial likelihood of success" and generalists with broad experience who can connect pieces of knowledge from disparate fields into new combinations and for new applications.

The most successful innovation team I've ever worked with was tasked with designing a new curriculum for a subject and grade level not currently served by the company. As straightforward as the effort initially seemed, we quickly ran into complex situations and no-win scenarios. In fact, the first question we had to answer—whether or not to include the Pythagorean theorem—was both complex and no-win.

Sierra, the team lead for the "print first, digital second" endeavor, was pulled from the digital design group but had experience in print products. Supporting her were four additional people:

- An editor with deep expertise in textbook publishing and a long tenure at the company

- A project manager and a graphic designer, both with industry experience but less than a year at the company

- A UX researcher with strong functional experience in multiple industries and nearly two years of experience conducting research at the current company

This level of diversity is either a source of incredible strength or debilitating tension within teams. Sierra turned it into a superpower.

When confronted with the Pythagorean theorem question, the answer seemed obvious—it should be included. This answer was reinforced by the project manager's research showing that it was required for an eighth grade textbook but optional for ninth grade. However, including it required the authors to write additional lessons, work not accounted for in the timeline, and it would add extra pages, a design decision that would push the book's price well above school districts' willingness and ability to pay. As the team debated and the issue was escalated up the ranks, Sierra went out of her way to encourage debate, celebrate the team's differences, and highlight the value of their opposing opinions. When the decision was finally made to include the Pythagorean theorem (and hire freelance writers and rethink design), it was obvious to everyone that Sierra had established a collaborative culture where teammates were encouraged to work through their differences and jointly propose solutions rather than elevating disagreements to the next level in the hierarchy and expecting them to resolve issues.

One more thing—even if you pick the perfect team, it's not enough to give them a strategy and a list of responsibilities and send them to work. They're people, not wind-up toys. Treat them like individuals and unite them as a team—one entity dedicated to innovation. We'll talk about how to do that in the next chapter.

How Will You Get There?

I had a client who *hated* the word "process" because they perceived it as describing an inviolable set of rules that eliminated the possibility of creativity and change. When I said we needed an innovation process, I'm pretty sure three of the five people on the team instantly broke out in hives. After much discussion, we started calling it our innovation playbook. The activities, phases, metrics, and timelines stayed the same, but if we hadn't changed the name, no one would have ever used it.

Your team has a more significant impact on your success than your process, and your process is only as effective as the decision-makers (that's you) who oversee it. It doesn't matter what you call it: you still need an innovation process because it guides what your team does, pointing to what happens next and what needs to happen before something else occurs, and it sets stakeholder expectations for the type and timing of results.

Every member of the innovation industrial complex has a process that promises to fulfill your innovation dreams. Companies spend lavishly to access the newest and shiniest one, hoping it is the perfect process. News flash: there is no perfect process.

News flash:
there is no
perfect process.

Innovation isn't baking. There's no recipe that, if followed precisely, results in the lightest, fluffiest, chocolatiest, butteriest, sweet but not too sweet chocolate chip cookie, which if altered by even the slightest granule of sugar leads to devastation. Innovation is stovetop cooking: as long as you have the essential ingredients, you can add, subtract, and experiment all you want.

Here are the essential steps:

1 **Diagnose:** Find a market opportunity or customer problem that is important and painful enough that it needs to be solved and big enough to be worth your while.

2 **Design:** Brainstorm a long and diverse list of possible solutions and business models and prioritize three to five of them for immediate prototyping and testing.

3 **Develop:** Experiment and refine solutions until you find the one that solves the problem, that the customer is willing to pay for, and that you can make money offering.

4 **De-risk:** Reduce the risk of a full launch by testing the critical desirability, viability, and feasibility assumptions in a real-world setting.

5 **Deliver:** Launch the innovation and begin to scale.

You can change everything about this process except for the order of the steps.* That means you can change the following:

---

* In a pinch, you can reverse the order of design (step 2) and diagnose (step 1), but you can't skip diagnose completely because it is the step that ensures that your solution creates value (i.e., meets the criteria to be innovation). Also, you may need to cycle through steps 2, 3, and 4 a few times before moving on to step 5.

- Name of the steps
- Specific activities
- People involved
- Criteria to move to the next step
- Expected timeline for each step

As with other elements of architecture, don't labor over this trying to find the exact combination of words, images, and metrics. Come up with the essentials, but don't worry about perfecting them before you get started, because things change. Pick a starting point; agree on activities, metrics, and timing; and then use it. You'll quickly learn what is missing, what confuses people, and what is unnecessarily onerous. As Sir Richard Branson said, "You don't learn to walk by following the rules. You learn to walk by trying and falling down."

Your process will evolve, but how you communicate it shouldn't. Before you show your process to someone, make sure it is excruciatingly clear that the process is not linear. At best, it's iterative. Usually, it looks and feels like this:

This image won't inspire confidence because all senior executives see is chaos without a timeline.

Win back their confidence with a nice, neat diagram like this:

DIAGNOSE the problem / DESIGN multiple ideas / DEVELOP solutions / DE-RISK the solution / DELIVER the value

Of course, that means that every time you show the process to someone, you'll have to remind them that it's iterative, not linear, more akin to an infinite loop with exit points at each step, and that not every project can or should complete all the steps. A linear diagram isn't perfect, but it's better than losing people's confidence and facing resistance before your work starts.

Building your strategy, team, and process is challenging and exhausting work. Even if, like Hope, you get everything set up in the first three months, don't be surprised when you spend the next nine revising and adapting it based on what you learn. That's normal. In fact, it's great, because you are learning and adapting your way to your own best practices.

Your behavior and architecture work comprises 80 percent of your time, energy, and effort in year 1. Defining and embedding the innovation culture in your team is the remaining 20 percent.

TL;DR Year 1 Architecture

You know an organization's priorities by how it allocates its resources. If your organization doesn't allocate resources to innovation, it isn't a priority. It's a hobby.

Start by setting an innovation strategy to make it clear to your stakeholders why innovation is essential and, more importantly, what's in it for them when they support it.

- State the problem(s) that innovation solves.
- Quantify the value it delivers (dollars and cents, baby).
- Make it obvious what the organization will and won't do.

Choose your team carefully. No matter how brilliant your strategy or process, you won't get the results you need if you have the wrong team.

- Have at least two people *plus you* on the team.
- Choose insiders and outsiders, experts and generalists to maximize creativity and practicality.
- Dedicate people full-time to innovation. No dotted line reporting and no 20 percent time.

Start working toward your goals by defining an innovation process that sets clear expectations, roles, and responsibilities.

- Define a process that starts by defining the problem, requires customer empathy, encourages expansive thinking, and mandates experimentation.
- Don't waste time searching for the perfect process or polishing the one you made. Use what you have, and refine it as you go.
- Remember (and remind others) that the process isn't linear. It's iterative.

Know Your Innovation Frameworks

IF I HAD a dime for every executive who asked me if we were using design thinking or agile, I could buy an island and move there so that I never have to answer if we're using design thinking or agile again. But I don't have an island, so the next best thing is helping you educate your stakeholders about the frameworks they read about and how you will or won't use them in your process.

To do that, here's a quick cheat sheet of the most popular innovation frameworks.

Human-Centered Design (also known as Design Thinking)

What it is: A problem-solving framework that integrates the needs of people, the possibilities of technology, and the requirements for business success grounded in three principles.

1 Inspiration: Understand customer needs.
2 Ideation: Generate creative ideas.
3 Iteration: Rapidly prototype and test.

Why it is important: Useful in solving "wicked problems," problems that are ill-defined or tricky and for which preexisting rules and domain knowledge is of limited or no help (or potentially detrimental).

When to use it: It's absolutely critical in the early stages of the process when you need to identify a customer problem or market opportunity as the focus of your innovation efforts. It should also be used throughout the innovation process to solicit feedback from consumers, customers, suppliers, and other key stakeholders.

How you do it:

- Qualitative research with tools like ethnography and Jobs to Be Done to build empathy with the customer
- Ideation to identify and explore lots of possible solutions
- Prototypes to build, test, and refine solutions

System Design

What it is: A way of making sense of the world's complexity by looking at it in terms of wholes and relationships rather than by splitting it down into its parts, grounded in five principles.

1 Acknowledge the interrelatedness of problems.

2 Develop empathy with the system.

3 Strengthen human relationships to enable creativity and learning.

4 Influence mental models to facilitate change.

5 Adopt an evolutionary design approach to desired systemic change.

Why it is important: The increased complexity caused by globalization, migration, and sustainability renders traditional design methods insufficient and increases the risk that designs result in unintended side effects.

When to use it:

- After initial market and/or customer discovery, ensure that you have captured inputs from all key stakeholders and understand key factors that could accelerate, maintain, or slow down the development of an opportunity space.

- After solution design and throughout prototyping, identify key constituents who should provide input on your proposed solution.

- When preparing for launch, ensure that you are engaging all key stakeholders in ways that accelerate, ease, or do not impede launch and scale efforts.

How you do it: This is an emerging innovation discipline with multiple schools of thought and dozens of potential tools. To learn more and find tools, check out the Systemic Design Association.

User Experience (UX) Design

What it is: A framework in which usability goals, user characteristics, environment, tasks, and workflow of a product, service, or process are given extensive attention at each stage of the design process and grounded in six principles.

1 Design is based upon an explicit understanding of users, tasks, and environments.

2 Users are involved throughout design and development.

3 Design is driven and refined by user-centered evaluation.

4 Process is iterative.

5 Design addresses the whole user experience.

6 Design team includes multidisciplinary skills and perspectives.

Why it is important: It optimizes the product around how users can, want, or need to use it so that users are not forced to change their behaviors and expectations to accommodate the product.

When to use it: After initial brainstorming is complete and multiple potential solutions are prioritized and prototyped.

How you do it: Personas, scenarios, and use cases that capture the context, behaviors, habits, and instincts that describe and drive user actions and choices.

Lean Startup

What it is: A methodology for developing businesses and products that emphasizes customer feedback over intuition and values flexibility over planning, grounded in five principles.

1 Entrepreneurs are everywhere
2 Entrepreneurship is management
3 Validated learning
4 Innovation accounting
5 Build-measure-learn

Why it is important: It aims to shorten product development cycles and rapidly discover if a proposed business model is viable.

When to use it: Beginning with initial rough prototypes and extending through to final product design and launch planning.

How you do it: The most common tools are

- Canvases: business model and value proposition
- Minimum viable product (MVP)
- Metrics that show causation and are actionable (versus ones that feel good but don't guide you to what's next)
- Innovation accounting
- Build-measure-learn loop, including A/B testing

Agile

What it is: A project management philosophy that expanded to be used in innovation and business transformation with four key principles.

1 Individuals and interactions over processes and tools
2 Working software over comprehensive documentation
3 Customer collaboration over contract negotiation
4 Responding to change over following a plan

Why it is important: It improves time to market, quality, and employee morale.

When to use it: Beginning with initial rough prototypes and extending through to final product design and launch planning.

How you do it: The most common tools are

- Agile teams that are small, entrepreneurial, and empowered
- Process and decision-making models with a focus on leadership and culture, management systems, structures, talent, and activities

Bringing It All Together

By now, you've probably noticed that these frameworks are very similar: many are centered on the customer, value diverse experience and expertise when creating solutions, and prioritize iteration over perfection. You've probably also noticed that each one aligns with one or more of the historical components of innovation processes.

- Market pull: design thinking
- External feedback: design thinking, system design, UX design, lean startup, agile
- External expertise and assistance: system design

Now that you have a basic framework, you still have the matter of the stakeholder asking if you're using the latest and greatest innovation process. You are, but you must connect the dots between your framework and the one your enthusiastic colleagues read about. Here's how they fit together:

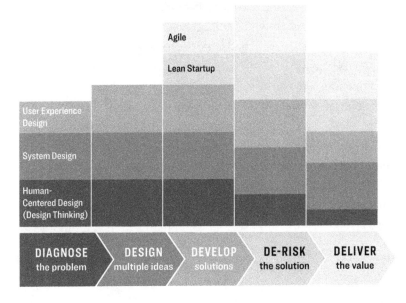

The thicker the shaded band in a column, the better suited the innovation framework is for the phase in the process. For example, human-centered design is excellent for diagnose, design, and develop phases; useful in de-risk; and okay in deliver. In contrast, agile is not suited for diagnose and design but is excellent for de-risk and deliver.

In diagnose and design, lean heavily on human-centered design because it keeps you open to all the types of people involved in the problem and the solution (not just users). If you're operating in a complex environment, like health care or education, bring in system design thinking to ensure you don't miss non-human elements like regulation, technology, or geopolitical dynamics that could significantly affect the problem and eventual solution.

In develop, start weaving in elements of lean startup, mainly its focus on building business models and not just individual products or services. Tools like the business model canvas are a huge help here and reveal critical but non-product or service assumptions that need to be tested.

In de-risk, lean startup and agile become (relatively) interchangeable, so use the language that best resonates within your organization. The key here is to apply the scientific method to your solution through rapid prototyping and testing.

In deliver, you've launched your solution, aiming to scale. Agile is designed for this, but keeping the human/user at the center of continuous improvement efforts is essential.

The key thing to remember is that you don't need to use any single specific framework. Instead, use a combination that works for you, your team's purpose, and your organization's culture.

Culture
Toolkit, Team, and Values

NORTHWEST ARKANSAS is a funny place. I loved almost every minute I lived there, working on P&G's Walmart sales team. *Almost* every minute. The minutes I didn't love, however, were the minutes when I learned the most.

A few months after I moved to Arkansas, a salesperson I worked with invited me to join him for a meeting with the buyer at Walmart's headquarters to present our category marketing plan. As we walked into the offices, it was clear this meeting would be very different from the ad agency meetings I was used to.

The vendor meeting area reminded me of my high school gym in both decor and smell. After being welcomed by a Walmart greeter, we selected our seats from the dozen metal folding chairs lining the walls and waited for the buyer to retrieve us. When he finally waved us in, we followed him down concrete hallways with flickering fluorescent lights to a windowless cinderblock room containing a folding table, four metal folding chairs, and an eight-by-ten framed photograph of company founder Sam Walton.

After we laid out our marketing plans and the sales and profit increases we expected it to drive, the buyer took a deep breath, looked at me, and said, "You seem like a sweet girl. Come with me." He stood and walked out of the room. I followed, grateful to hear my colleague's footsteps behind me.

Back down the concrete hallway, through the high school gym/ waiting area, past the greeter, and into the parking lot we went, stopping only once we reached the sidewalk. He pointed across the street to the Walmart Supercenter and said, "Do you see what it says on that building? Right under the Walmart name?"

"It says 'Always Low Prices. Always,'" I replied, my voice lilting up, making it more like a question than a statement.

"Exactly. 'Always Low Prices.' All that money you put into making those pretty pictures and all the money you'll spend on your fancy marketing plan is money you could use to lower the cost of your products. Come back when you understand what we do and what we care about." Then with a curt nod and heel spin, he walked away.

In those minutes, I learned Walmart's culture.

Over the next year, I would experience more of the company's culture—seven a.m. Saturday morning meetings, a star-studded shareholders meeting that filled the University of Arkansas basketball arena, and the "joy" of working side by side with my colleagues to scrape fossilized laundry detergent off store shelves before reorganizing how products were displayed. But none of those experiences are as real and vivid in my memory as the minutes outside Walmart's headquarters.

In your role, you have the same power to make an impression and communicate a culture as the Walmart buyer did. You also have a responsibility to create the culture you want for innovation.

What Is Culture?

My favorite answer to this question is that culture is like pornography: you know it when you see it.* However, as amusing and memorable as that answer is, it's not helpful when describing an existing culture or establishing a new one. For those purposes, I find this definition far more useful:

> An organization's culture is a system of shared meaning based on employees' perceptions of the organization's values and available toolkit.

There's a lot there, so let's unpack it:

- **System** refers to the fact that culture comprises many different things, including people, practices, places, and objectives.

- **Shared meaning** reflects the fact that the meanings of the system and its components must be shared across the people in the organization.

- **Perception** is nonevaluative. Culture reflects what people see, hear, and experience, not whether or not they like or dislike what they see, hear, and experience.

---

* This is a reference to the famous 1964 Supreme Court case *Jacobellis v. Ohio* (378 U.S. 184). Nico Jacobellis, the owner of a Cleveland-area theater, was convicted on two counts of possessing and exhibiting an obscene film. He appealed his conviction all the way up to the Supreme Court, claiming that the film in question was not obscene, so it was constitutionally protected under the First Amendment. The court found in his favor, and Justice Potter Stewart, in support of the court's finding, famously wrote, "I shall not today attempt further to define the kinds of material I understand to be embraced within that shorthand description; and perhaps I could never succeed in intelligibly doing so. *But I know it when I see it*, and the motion picture involved in this case is not that." (Emphasis added.)

An organization's culture is a system of shared meaning based on employees' perceptions of the organization's values and available toolkit.

- **Values** are what we prefer, want, and cherish, defining both what we want and the acceptable means through which to attain those goals.

- **Toolkit** encompasses the processes, stories, rituals, artifacts, and other assets we can use to understand something or take action.

As a leader, you can control some aspects of the system and the toolkit through the strategies and processes you put in place. You can influence the values, how they're perceived, and how widely they're shared through your words and actions.

The bottom line is that, yes, you'll know the culture when you see it—and hopefully it looks familiar because you helped create it.

You're Not Starting from Scratch

You're creating an innovation team within an existing organization, and understanding the organization's existing culture is critical to how you think about building the innovation culture. You're also working with different people and teams who have their own cultures, and understanding and working with those cultures is also critical to gaining buy-in and support for your work.

In a review and meta-analysis of "more than 100 of the most commonly used social and behavioral models," Harvard Business School professor Boris Groysberg and his colleagues made two fascinating discoveries. First, they identified two aspects that determine an organization's culture regardless of its size, industry, type, or geography: the extent to which people interact and how people respond to change. Second, they identified eight cultures that are distinctly and measurably different in their styles, work environments, values, leadership emphasis, advantages, and disadvantages.

The two driving aspects of culture are combined to create a matrix against which each of the eight cultures can be plotted.

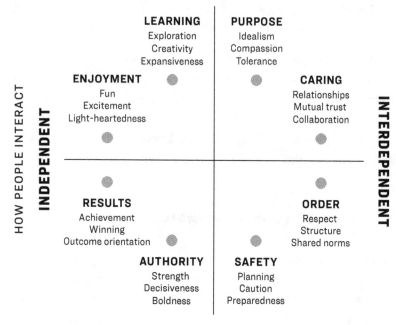

HOW PEOPLE RESPOND TO CHANGE

FLEXIBILITY

LEARNING | **PURPOSE**
Exploration | Idealism
Creativity | Compassion
Expansiveness | Tolerance

ENJOYMENT | **CARING**
Fun | Relationships
Excitement | Mutual trust
Light-heartedness | Collaboration

RESULTS | **ORDER**
Achievement | Respect
Winning | Structure
Outcome orientation | Shared norms

AUTHORITY | **SAFETY**
Strength | Planning
Decisiveness | Caution
Boldness | Preparedness

STABILITY

HOW PEOPLE INTERACT — **INDEPENDENT** — **INTERDEPENDENT**

Each quadrant conveniently contains two cultures that are similar to each other and able to coexist relatively peacefully with their neighbor in the adjacent quadrant. For example, a learning culture, characterized by exploration and creativity, is similar to a culture of enjoyment, characterized by fun and excitement, because they're nestled together in the independent (how people work together) and flexibility (how people respond to change) quadrant. A learning culture is also consistent with a culture of purpose, characterized by idealism and compassion, because they are the two cultures in which people are most flexible during times of change.

Problems start the further apart cultures are in the matrix. A person from a learning culture who is used to working independently and being flexible when things change feels tension and even discomfort when they encounter a safety culture characterized by planning and caution, in which people are more interdependent and seek stability.

Hope was lucky. Because she pulled her innovation team from an existing team, and they had all worked with her and with each other, there were very few culture clashes. That wasn't the case as her team worked with the BUs and other functional teams at MaXperience. For example, when her team and its learning culture initially began to work with manufacturing and its culture of safety and order, sparks flew. Hope's team felt like they were getting the runaround because when they asked someone in manufacturing for information, they were constantly referred to other people, a sign of the function's interdependent culture. Manufacturing, however, didn't initially trust Hope's team because they felt her team never gave them a definitive answer, missing the reality that Hope's team needed to maintain a flexible approach given the high-assumption, low-knowledge environment in which they operated. Once we diagnosed the clashing cultures, Hope's team approached manufacturing with more empathy and dedicated time to explaining why they were asking questions and why they couldn't give definitive answers. With a better understanding of the why behind Hope's team's requests and suggestions, manufacturing was better equipped to provide answers.

I'm telling you all this not because you need to embrace and use this framework (though you should check it out—I've used it, and it works) but to make the point that you need to know the cultures that are already in place in your organization before you jump into building your own. Jump too far, and you'll create tension, discomfort, and even resistance with others in the core business and key stakeholders. Don't jump far enough, and the healthy tension that's one of the first signs of growth may not occur.

You *Are* Starting Your Team's Culture from Scratch

With full knowledge of your starting point—your organization's existing culture—you can now make a fully informed decision about the innovation culture you want to build, starting with your team.

In his seminal paper "The Role of the Founder in Creating Organizational Culture," MIT professor Edgar Schein cuts straight to the point: "The founder of an organization simultaneously creates an [organization] and, by force of his or her personality, begins to shape the culture of that group." He goes on to list the ten "mechanisms" a founder has in their culture-creation toolkit:

1 Formal statements, like mission, vision, and values

2 Design of physical space, including the location of buildings and office layouts

3 Leadership behaviors like role modeling, teaching, and coaching

4 Incentive and reward systems, including compensation models and promotion criteria

5 Stories, legends, myths, and parables about people and events

6 Governance systems, including what managers pay attention to, measure, and control

7 Manager reactions to unexpected events, critical incidents, and crises

8 Organizational design and structure, including the degree of decentralization

9 Standard systems and processes for evaluation, analysis, and decision-making

10 Performance evaluation criteria in recruitment, hiring, promotion, leveling off, and firing

All of these things are in place in your organization, and they define the culture you're in. Look around your organization and note how many of these tools you see. Are there conference room posters with the organization's mission, vision, and values? What leadership behaviors are recognized and reinforced? How are the offices set up? What do the performance evaluation and incentive systems reward?

Few of these things are in place for your innovation team. As its founder, you create them and use them to shape the innovation culture within your team and, eventually, the broader organization.

Good news: just like Hope with her white paper, you started doing just that when you worked on your leadership behaviors in chapter 4 and the innovation process in chapter 5. Only one more thing to do (on this topic, this year).

Hope also designed a dedicated innovation space in an abandoned wing of a company-owned building a few miles from headquarters. She wanted a space where the team would be free from interruptions from their former colleagues and the artifacts, branding, and marketing that defined the current company. She decorated the "Growth Gym" with IKEA furniture, flea market finds, and counterculture art and slogans. Then she called everyone together for a meeting.

Build the Culture with Your Team

People join your team for many reasons: some because they support the strategy, understand the process, and have the skills and experience to meet your expectations—and some because they were assigned to your team and are wondering what they have gotten themselves into. You need to make everyone a believer, but it's not enough for success. It's not enough to motivate people to take risks and run through brick walls, especially in years 2 and 3. To do that, they need to believe that their actions have a bigger purpose and move everyone closer to a greater goal. They need to believe you are the right person to lead them there, and then they will choose to follow you.

Before your team believes in you, they must trust you. Before they trust you, they need to know you. For them to know you, you need to be (dun, dun, dun) vulnerable (gasp!). Vulnerability is increasingly recognized as a critical leadership trait that results in greater trust, innovation, creativity, and growth within teams. The good news is that you can be vulnerable without sharing embarrassing stories or baring your soul.

Just like Hope did in the Growth Gym, gather your team together and share your motivations for taking this role and your aspirations for your career, your team's accomplishments, and your organization's growth. Then ask the team to share their motivations and aspirations. Ask them why they want to work on innovation, what they want to achieve in this role, and how they want to be known or remembered as a professional and as a person. Listen and ask questions. Resist the urge to jump in with advice or suggestions.

When everyone has shared, take a break for a few hours or days but no more than a week. During the break, reflect on what you heard. Find the common themes and note places where motivations and aspirations may conflict. Jot down your thoughts. Ask the team to jot down theirs. Nothing formal, no emails or slides or even complete sentences. Just handwritten thoughts on scraps of paper.

When you come back together, ask everyone to share what they jotted down and use those thoughts to brainstorm your team's shared values. At this point, defining your team's shared values is more important than determining the team's mission or vision, because your values drive your behaviors.

The team's shared values are nonnegotiable. They are your "Always Low Prices. Always." They permeate everything your team

The team's shared values are **nonnegotiable.**

does—how you talk to and work with people, how you make decisions, and how you are perceived and treated by others. The values don't have to be fancy or professionally wordsmithed. Some of the clearest and most compelling lists of shared values come from five-minute brain dumps. For example:

- Humans are at the center of everything we do.
- Progress is more important than perfection.
- If you learn something, you didn't fail.
- If we're not making mistakes, we're not pushing far enough.
- There is no "I" in team.
- We are stewards of the company first and foremost.

You'll know you're moving in the right direction when the team shouts "*Yes!*" and tells stories of times they've seen or done just that. You've nailed it when people outside the team react with either "Oh my goodness, yes! Sign me up!" or "Who in their right mind would want to be part of that?"

Consistency is key when it comes to shared values. You and your team need to demonstrate them every day in every interaction because everything you say and do becomes evidence of innovation's role within the organization. When you or someone on your team falls short (it's okay, no one's perfect), talk about it, understand why it happened, and discuss how to do better next time. Or you could print out your shared values in giant letters, tape them to the side of the office, drag your team outside, and tell them to read what it says on the side of the building.

Trust me, the culture will stick.

TL;DR Year 1 Culture

Culture is a system of shared meaning based on employees' perceptions. Create an innovation culture that pushes but doesn't pulverize the organization's culture.

Understand the broader organizational culture.

- Watch how people interact and respond to change. That's your organization's culture.
- Identify one or two cultures that best describe what you observe.
- Define the innovation culture you want while working with the broader organization's existing culture.

Define your innovation culture by using Schein's ten tools at your disposal as the founder of the innovation team.

- Clarify and refine leadership behaviors and team process, as described in previous chapters.
- Capture stories and rituals as they emerge.
- Guide the development of other tools, like performance evaluation and incentive and rewards systems, as they evolve in response to business changes.

Work with your team to establish and document the shared values that define your innovation culture.

- Share your aspirations and motivations with the team. Explain how they influence how you think, speak, and behave.
- Ask your team to share why they want to work on innovation, what they hope to achieve, and how they want to be known or remembered.
- Work together to draft a short list of nonnegotiable shared values.

Know Your Innovators.
Celebrate Your Operators

WHEN ORGANIZATIONS WANT to "be more innovative," executives often push the belief that "everyone is an innovator." This often manifests in innovation events like hackathons and shark tanks. It also tends to fuel the belief that an innovation role is required for promotion. People hear messages about innovation's importance, see how it affects every aspect of the business, and believe it is the best way to demonstrate their leadership potential and catapult their careers into the stratosphere.

It's true. For some people. For others, it's a one-way ticket to frustration, doubt, and regret. For these people, a stint in innovation is a tragedy because self-doubt often motivates them to leave the company, even though they're *exactly* the people you want and need running your current business.

Luckily, this situation can be avoided by communicating one very simple message over and over and over: Operators *and* innovators are equally important, equally essential, and equally loved.

Of course, this message becomes infinitely more believable if you reinforce it through actions. Here are a few of the more effective ones I've seen.

Project Agnostic Promotion Criteria

When I was at P&G, it was common knowledge that to be promoted to brand manager, you had to launch a line extension. This was easy to do on an existing brand but very hard to do on an innovation team that hadn't even launched a base brand. Understandably, performance and promotion criteria were geared toward what P&G did most frequently and struggled to accommodate activities and achievements outside that mold.

A better approach is to go one step deeper and assess performance not on *what* the work is but rather on *how* it gets done—for example, your ability to lead, manage, or work with a cross-functional team, manage the budget, communicate with senior leaders, etc. Because all these skills are required in operations and innovation, it's easier to show people a path to a promotion that fits their skills rather than one that conforms to organizational rumors or personal beliefs.

Celebrate the Operators

It can feel like innovators get all the love. After all, who is more likely to be celebrated onstage at the shareholder's meeting or company-wide town hall: the team that just launched a new product or the team that reduced expense report approvals from five days to four?

But the fact is operators—especially those focused on doing things better, faster, and cheaper—make innovators' work possible. Without ongoing improvements to existing processes, the company would soon lag behind competitors, losing operational advantages and loyal customers. Without their work, there is no budget or runway for innovation.

For every innovator or innovation project you celebrate, celebrate an operator or process improvement project. Make a big deal, shower them with confetti, and give them a round of applause. They deserve it.

Listen, Ask, Act

It is perhaps the simplest yet most impactful thing you can do: listen to suggestions, ask questions to understand why it's important and how it helps, then act on the tip or explain why you won't.

People are full of ideas but learn not to share them because they see what happens when others do—they're ignored, pacified, or punished. Eventually, you start to hear murmurs of "I've been saying for years that we should . . ." and "If only they listened to me back in . . ." and "I don't want to say I told you so, but I told you so."

So, start listening. When people bring you an idea, get curious and ask questions to understand why they think this is the right thing to do for the business. Maybe they're right and have hit on a huge potential improvement or cost savings. Act on it. Maybe they're right, but the idea is too small or requires more resources than it's worth. Tell them why you won't act on it.

People want to feel heard. They feel valued when they know they have been.

YEAR TWO

7

Faith

FAITH HAD held every innovation role imaginable—founder, funder, consultant, and team member. But after leading a corporate innovation team in her last role, she swore she would never again work in a big company. Instead, she returned to her beloved startup scene, advising and mentoring founders, passing time until she found another problem to fall in love with. But in the back of her mind was the lesson she worked so hard to teach: just because your first attempt failed doesn't mean it's impossible; it means you learned and increased the odds of future success.

So when the next big company opportunity came, Faith couldn't resist trying again. This time it was at Ninjacorn Financial Services (NFS), one of the largest financial institutions in the world.

Like in her first experience, Faith would take over an existing team with ongoing projects. But while management at her previous job had no idea that the projects underway were failing and the team was baffled by how to fix them, her new boss, John, was heavily involved in the projects and confident that they were on track. He was also convinced he had the right team, having overseen its expansion from thirty to over one hundred people in just one year to support its rapidly growing project portfolio.

Another significant difference was the role Faith would play. In her first experience, she oversaw all innovation activities, but in this role, she would lead one of several innovation teams and act as a key advisor to John, the executive in charge of innovation. John's team was centralized, not bound to a specific BU or line of operations, and reported directly to the CEO. This was in stark contrast with her first team, which sat within an existing business unit and competed with the core business for resources and the BU president's time and attention.

As Faith moved her belongings to her new home in a new city, she felt confident that she had asked all the right questions to learn what she needed to know to prepare for her new role. At the very least, she reasoned, she knew what she didn't know and could figure out the rest.

It wasn't long before she figured out, as the saying goes, "It ain't what you don't know that hurts you. It's what you know for sure that just ain't so."

Quick Wins

During Faith's first weeks in her new job, she discovered that what John knew for sure wasn't so and was about to hurt them. As year 2 dawned for the team, projects that at first glance appeared on track were in fact woefully behind schedule or entirely off the rails. People were working on projects that John didn't approve of, and because he was unaware of this, he frequently volunteered his teams to work on every new idea and request that crossed his desk.

Further compounding issues was a culture of FOMO (fear of missing out) that had grown over the past year, making everyone believe they needed to be involved in every project. Teams ballooned to over forty members, and people reported spending fifty or more hours each week in meetings. Even the innovation process and language established in the team's early days to help them work more efficiently had become vague memories referenced by only a few "old-timers."

"It was a perfect example of activity mistaken for achievement," Faith reflected. "Over one hundred people, deeply committed to the mission of the company and the team, working insane hours and trying desperately to do the right thing. But the more they did, the less progress they made."

Despite John's strong bond with the CEO, Faith knew the clock was ticking. The team needed meaningful results to maintain their current funding level... and keep their jobs.

The team needed quick wins, small projects that produced tangible results and acted as evidence of the team's ability to deliver on its goals. Faith tasked one of her direct reports with interviewing every member of the hundred-plus innovation team and compiling a list of potential quick wins. The resulting report highlighted dozens of opportunities, everything from process improvements to leadership and cultural changes. However, three possible quick wins stood out: reducing the time spent in meetings, improving the onboarding process for new team members, and clarifying roles and responsibilities.

Initially hesitant to acknowledge the flaws in his team, John quickly relented when the results of an enterprise-wide, team-specific employee satisfaction survey confirmed the interview findings. With his vocal support, Faith quickly assembled small working groups and gave them six months to develop and implement solutions for each quick win opportunity.

Less Is More

Everyone knew the team was working on too many things, but no one would stop working on anything. Every project could be justified, rationalized, and defended. Every project was important to someone, and no one wanted to be the meanie who called a project unimportant. Relationships were currency in the company's culture, and attempting to shut down a project would cost you dearly.

But there's a difference between being mean and being honest.

The team needed to learn and practice the difference. Faith knew that doing so required a way to evaluate projects objectively, so she set to work defining the team's innovation playground—a set of parameters and metrics to assess the strategic fit, financial impact, and operational implications of a wide variety of projects in various stages of development.

As her quick wins teams worked to implement changes, Faith developed, socialized, and refined the playground's prioritization parameters for two months. In her first test of their usefulness and accuracy, she applied them to three projects—one that had been shut down, one in progress, and one that was a very early and ill-defined idea. The parameters didn't produce the expected results. So, she made changes and tried again. It took several more rounds of revisions and applications of the parameters to a growing number of projects before Faith had a tool that could withstand the leadership team's scrutiny. As word of the innovation playground got out, she heard rumors that she was building a decision machine, and there were whispers of resistance to being dictated to by a spreadsheet. Even though she was still testing and experimenting, Faith realized she also needed to share her work and communicate its purpose—she was building a tool to facilitate conversations, not spit out decisions. The goal wasn't to shut down projects; it was to help focus the team on the highest-impact work.

After months of work, Faith and John shared the tool with the CEO. He loved it.

The next day, teams started using it to evaluate their projects.

By the end of the month, the entire team acknowledged its impact on their work and mental health. By applying the tool, the team moved from reactive to responsive, and reports of burnout plummeted. They no longer addressed issues after they arose, acting impulsively and changing decisions based on the latest input. Instead, they considered things within the broader context of the innovation team's work, discussed trade-offs, and adapted thoughtfully to major challenges.

Recommitting to Values

There's a unique joy in being part of a founding team in year 1. You're bonded by your shared faith in an idea and the shared experience of turning that idea into something real and tangible. You faced doubt and setbacks together. You have skin in the game and your hearts on the line. You're more like parents than owners. As the team grows, the bonds stretch. If it grows too quickly, they snap. Inevitably, the shared faith and experience fade and are replaced with new perceptions and experiences. It's normal, but it still hurts.

That's why they're called growing pains. Not growing tickles.

Now in year 2, the innovation team was in pain. The interview and survey results that kicked off the quick wins teams pointed to a deeper and far more difficult to fix issue: lack of trust. Over the course of year 1, trust eroded due to vague communication, poor collaboration among people and teams, and perceived lack of accountability for behaving according to the team's original shared values and ways of working. People regularly canceled plans at the last minute, even if their absence delayed a critical decision or stalled a project. Faith's peers on the leadership team routinely made commitments in meetings only to later tell their teams that it was okay not to deliver if they had more important things to do.

Faith knew that rebuilding trust took time, but it wouldn't happen if no one took the time to address the issue. So, she enrolled her peers and HR partners in a slow but steady process of defining

That's why they're called growing pains. **Not growing tickles.**

the team's ways of working. Through professionally facilitated con-versations, the team worked to understand each person's habits and preferences better, develop team norms, recommit to shared values, and resolve issues in real time.

As months ticked by, the team's behavior improved, improving effectiveness along with it. With new ways of working in place and reinforced shared values, team members felt empowered to ask questions and call out bad behavior. They also felt more comfort-able having conversations to clarify roles and expectations, ask for help, and work through problems together.

Onward and Outward

With quick wins producing results, and the team increasingly focused on fewer higher-impact projects, with greater respect and trust in each other, Faith turned her attention to replenishing the portfolio as projects progressed and others paused or were canceled. She knew from experience that even with the team fully consumed by the existing project load, they would soon need new problems to solve.

Faith tapped two people and an external expert to be her scouts. She instructed them to look within and beyond their industry. She told them to investigate new inventions and technologies, even if they were only hypotheses in academic labs. She asked them to scout startups and talk to people on the fringes, not well-known experts. She wanted her team to bring back ideas and insights that surprised her and made the company uncomfortable. She expected disruption and wanted her scouts to lead the way.

She also needed a way to scout for ideas and insights within the company. Faith knew that, like at most large companies, because most employees were in operational roles, focused solely on doing their jobs and serving their customers to the best of their abilities, ideas stayed trapped in their heads. And that was a problem because employees in operational roles saw problems no one else saw and had ideas for fixing them. They could be innovators, too, if someone would just let them.

John and the CEO knew this, too, and feared that they were missing out on big ideas. Starting on her very first day, they pressured Faith to install an idea collection system. For nine months, she pushed back. She wanted to give everyone an opportunity to share their ideas, but she knew from experience that opening the system to everyone would crush the innovation team under the weight of tens of thousands of ideas.

To build the enterprise-wide innovation culture the CEO wanted, each idea needed to be evaluated using objective criteria. Each submission required a thoughtful response with results of the idea's evaluation and suggestions for improvement. If the system was a black box, it would become a joke, evidence of a management team that says one thing but does another. To get the big ideas NFS wanted, people needed to understand what "big" looked like.

Faith and her team took the same approach to idea collection as they took to all their projects: they started small. They identified a few locations and teams with a history of thinking big and running experiments. They prototyped a simple, homemade system to collect ideas, evaluate them using the innovation playground, and provide personalized feedback. The team asked users for feedback on the process, system, and experience and refined the prototype as they went. As Faith and her team iterated, the buzz across locations grew. People clamored for access and, more importantly, began to understand the types and sizes of ideas worth submitting. Year 3 was the right time to go enterprise-wide with a purpose-built system.

The Results

By the end of the innovation team's second year, they operated like a well-oiled machine.

Thanks to a portfolio of fewer but higher-impact projects, people were no longer on the brink of burnout. Roles and responsibilities were clear again, and the team members felt comfortable asking questions and requesting help in accordance with their shared values. Time spent in meetings was half of what it was at the beginning of the year, giving people time to work together and make meaningful progress on their projects.

Most importantly, when the year ended, the team delivered measurable results: higher employee engagement, lower turnover, and a portfolio of projects on track and ready to generate revenue starting in year 3.

8

Behavior
Inspiration and Hard Conversations

I'M REASONABLY SURE that no one has ever accused Vanilla Ice of being a management guru. But his classic song, "Ice Ice Baby," contains a nugget of wisdom that every leader should adopt: stop, collaborate, and listen.

That's precisely what you need to do at the start of year 2.

This year, you have three big priorities: delivering results, leading and managing your team, and expanding innovation's influence in the organization. The following two chapters dig into how to get short-term results from long-term investments and spread innovation's influence without abandoning your team. This chapter is where you'll plan the behaviors that enable you to be the leader and manager your team needs this year.

But first, you need to stop, collaborate, and listen. Oh, and get out your pen and paper, because I'm going to ask you some questions soon.

Stop (or at Least Pause)

Time is your most precious resource. It is scarce and finite. Once it's gone, it's gone forever. Everyone wants your time. They *need* it. It's easy to believe the desperate pleas, the panicked calls, and spur-of-the-moment meeting invites. Emergencies need to be dealt with immediately. But real emergencies are rare. Usually, what we call emergencies are unexpected situations that can wait an hour or a day until we have the time and mind space to tackle them.

Think about the last time something unexpected happened—your water heater died in the middle of winter, your kid got pink eye and couldn't go to school, or a light bulb burned out. The first two are emergencies, so you immediately dealt with them and moved other things down the priority list. The light bulb is annoying, but you didn't rearrange your day to put a new one in. You made a mental note to change it when you had time.

As researcher and author Laura Vanderkam explained in her TED Talk, "'I don't have time' means 'It's not a priority.'"

Stopping takes time.

It's also a priority if you want to grow as a leader.

Think back to your school days and how you learned. Your teacher stood in front of the classroom, said a bunch of stuff, and then you practiced applying what you heard through classroom activities and homework assignments. A few weeks or months later, you took a test to determine how well you learned or memorized the materials.

Now think about your life and your work since school. You don't sit in a classroom, have people tell you how to do things, and then practice those things in a pleasant, safe environment with few to no consequences. You get thrown into something, make mistakes, learn something, and eventually you figure it out. You learn by doing, and you improve by reflecting on the results of your doing.

Reflection is vital to learning and growing as a leader.

It takes time, but it's a priority if you want to succeed.

Reflection is vital to learning and growing as a leader. **It takes time, but it's a priority if you want to succeed.**

Look Back: How You Spent Your Time

How you choose to spend your time reflects your priorities. Look back at where you spent your time last year. Did you spend it on activities that moved you closer to your aspirations, or were you primarily reacting to your circumstances? Did you give in to the instincts that made you a great operator, or did you engage in behaviors that initially felt uncomfortable but encouraged and supported innovation? If how you spent your time and energy last year reflects your priorities, that's great! For most of us, it doesn't.

When you cancel a meeting, drop out of a research trip, step out of a brainstorming session, or reschedule a progress update, you usually explain that it's because you don't have time. What the team hears is that it's not a priority. And that may be true at that moment. But if it became a habit over the last year or you didn't explain why you don't have time, you're telling the team and the rest of the organization that innovation is not a priority.

With the benefit of a year's worth of observations, experiences, and data, consider the context you're now innovating in. What's changed in the world and your company since the start of last year? Is the change permanent, or is it more of a blip? Seeing the big picture and understanding if and how it's changed helps ensure you're calmly and rationally evaluating the situation and not emotionally reacting based on a recent event.

Consider your aspirations, instincts, and behaviors. Were they consistent with who you wanted to be as an innovation leader last year? Is that still the leader you want and need to be this year? Or have your aspirations changed? If they have, why, what are they now, and what behavior do you need to change to achieve them?

There were no right or wrong answers a year ago when you thought about your instincts, your organization's identity, who you wanted to be as a leader, and what you wanted to work on. And there are no right or wrong answers now—only honest and dishonest ones.

The honest ones sustain and guide you through the work and challenges ahead. The dishonest answers, or the ones you should make time for but don't, keep you stuck where you are.

Look Around: Your Team

You already know that your team makes or breaks your success. How are they doing? What time are you spending with them? Are they still living the shared values, or have they slipped back into old habits and ways of working? Are they still committed to the team's mission and goals, or are they so heads-down in their work that they no longer see the big picture?

John's team definitely fell back into old habits and lost sight of the big picture as they became overwhelmed and consumed by their individual responsibilities. It took a fresh set of eyes and new thinking from Faith to see the problem and fix it. This situation is more common than people want to admit.

When a leading food and beverage company decided to reprioritize innovation after several years of focus on process optimization, people were excited. The president and the VPs that reported to him spent three months developing an innovation strategy, process, and detailed metrics. They discussed their instincts during that time and agreed to do the opposite. They committed to each other that they would resist the urge to demand detailed financial forecasts and sourcing and manufacturing plans. They promised to focus first on learning and building instincts to ask questions about the problems to be solved, consumer feedback on ideas, and other elements critical to ensuring early stage concepts' desirability, feasibility, and financial viability. It would be a significant behavior change for everyone, but they committed to making it.

Thirty days later, the newly appointed innovation director, Kate, shared nine market opportunities with the president and the VPs.

She explained that all nine represented important and unsatisfied consumer problems and that three were especially ripe for exploration. In fact, Kate and her teammate had gone so far as to brainstorm ideas for each of the three areas, share the ideas with consumers, and collect feedback. Instead of responding with awe at her progress and asking why she selected the three she did, the VPs grilled her about raw material sourcing and costs, expected volume, and when samples would be ready for taste tests. They demanded detailed profit and loss projections and five-year net present value analysis. The president was surprised because this behavior was counter to their commitment, but he didn't say anything, afraid of embarrassing his direct reports.

A few days later, still bothered by his VPs' behavior, the president pulled Kate aside and apologized. "You did a great job," he said. He explained that the VPs' questions were out of line and completely inappropriate for the phase of work. He reassured her that she was doing the right things, that he was impressed by how much she had achieved in only a month, and that he had her back.

Month after month, this cycle repeated. Kate presented her progress. The VPs interrogated her about sourcing, manufacturing, and financial details. The president said nothing in the meeting but reassured Kate privately.

One year later, the first product launched right on schedule, and two others were in the pipeline. People across the company marveled at what Kate accomplished and asked her to teach them how to do it, but the VPs complained it took too long to get the details. In his year-end letter to the organization, the president wrote one sentence thanking Kate for her hard work. He penned paragraphs recognizing the VPs' accomplishments.

Eighteen months after she was hired, Kate quit. The innovation pipeline evaporated. The VPs were shocked. The president was flabbergasted. After all, he gave her so much support, and the VPs were just following their instincts.

If your team continues to behave in ways consistent with the team's mission and shared values, that's wonderful. But if they aren't, especially if the inconsistent behavior is becoming a habit, you need to hold them accountable. It isn't fun, but it is necessary. In fact, it's leadership.

Look Forward: Prioritize

Reflecting is surprisingly exhausting, so take a deep breath before you look ahead. Have a cup of tea (or something slightly more potent) and a chocolate chip cookie. Stare out the window. Allow yourself to breathe, and let your mind go blank or run wild for a few minutes. Your next plan is surprisingly better after you take a break than if you'd charged ahead, worried you don't have enough time to reflect.

At least once per year, gather your team together for some in-person bonding. Start by celebrating last year's accomplishments. Resist the urge to stand at the front of the room ticking down a list. Instead, make the celebration one that is by the team, for the team. Ask them to celebrate themselves, their teammates, and everyone else who helped during the past year. Then before you dive into planning the next year, go back to the beginning.

Return to your mission and shared values. Acknowledge that it's easy to lose sight of them during the stress and pressure of daily work but that you don't want this team to be where those words are, at best, aspirational. You want them to be lived. Then share stories of when you did and didn't live the values last year.

One of the more counterintuitive truisms of human nature is that the more you give, the more you receive. This is one of the foundational principles of improv, and I see it play out all the time in qualitative research—the more you share about yourself, about your inner world and feelings, the more people share with you. So, be open with your team. Share your reflections. Admit your imperfections. (News flash: your team knows you're not perfect. They've discussed it. A lot.)

Ask your team to reflect and write down (yes, by hand) when they have and haven't lived the shared values this year. Invite them to share their stories. Encourage them to share stories of when teammates lived the values. Then collaborate to reaffirm or revise the shared values.

Once you've recommitted, it's time to have the uncomfortable conversation. It's time to talk about accountability. This conversation is a buzzkill, especially after the warm fuzzies of celebrations and shared values. However, without accountability, all your work, reflections, conversations, and plans are nothing but words. Under stress, we become more ourselves. We fall back into old habits, thought patterns, and behaviors. Talking about accountability gives us permission to help each other minimize the time spent in old ways and maximize the time spent being who we want to be. It's also easier to talk about accountability when times are good.

Just like you did with the shared values conversation, start with yourself. Little is more perilous or fraught with danger than giving your boss feedback. You don't know how they'll react, or you do know and it's not pretty. You don't know if silence means reflection or it's merely the calm before the storm. You don't know if the quiet "thank you" is genuine or the last thing you hear before retribution commences.

As a vulnerable, self-aware, and inspiring leader, remove your team's fear by telling people what you want feedback on and how to give it to you. Commit to accepting it and asking questions if you don't understand it. Acknowledge the bravery required to be honest and reassure them that you are grateful, even if it may not always seem that way.

You can't be with your team every moment, and quite honestly, you shouldn't be. They need to work and create together, which requires constructively resolving conflicts. Achieving this requires holding each other accountable, so help them figure out how.

Ask your team how they want to be held accountable, not just by you but by each other. When I worked on P&G's Walmart sales team, a floor-to-ceiling poster was signed by all two hundred people on the team that read "Promises Made. Promises Kept." We knew that no matter what happened, if we made a promise, we were expected to keep it. It didn't matter if it was a significant promise like an annual revenue commitment or a small promise like returning a pen. You kept the promise. If you didn't, anyone on the team could call you out.

A manager holds people accountable for what they deliver.

A leader holds people accountable for *how* they deliver.

Anyone on your team can be a leader. Take the time to show them. It's a priority.

TL;DR Year 2 Behavior

If it's not worth your time, it's not a priority (and that may be okay, just be honest about it).

Reflect on how you spent your time.

- Did your choices reflect your priorities?
- How have the changes of the past year impacted your approach and aspirations?
- How is your progress toward becoming the innovation leader you want to be reflected in your behaviors and instincts?

Reflect on your team, their progress, and their behaviors.

- How much time are you spending with your team? How are you helping them make progress in their work and develop as leaders?
- What are examples of the team's shared values in action? What are examples of when the team fell a bit short?
- How are you holding yourself and your team accountable for delivering your goals and demonstrating your shared values?
- How did you acknowledge the team's big wins and small moments when your team demonstrated its shared values?

Look to the future and collaborate with your team on what comes next.

- Are you pursuing opportunities that support the organization's priorities and close the growth gap? If not, what needs to change?
- How are you holding each other accountable for making tangible progress toward achieving your innovation goals?

9

Architecture
Results, Priorities, and Decisions

MANY YEARS AGO, I was with an innovation team when they met with the CEO to formally kick off their work. As they laid out their strategy and plans for the coming months, the CEO nodded silently. Eventually, she couldn't hide her impatience and interrupted, "Look, ultimately we need a business that generates $250 million in the next two years. How are you going to do that?"

I burst out laughing. The team, all two of them, looked crestfallen.

"With all due respect," I said, trying to gather myself, "if we could do that, we wouldn't be sitting in this room with you. We'd be out doing that."

You are the founder and leader of the innovation team, but it ain't no bootstrapped startup. Your team is well funded thanks to your investors—the executives and shareholders who gave you the money and the head count you need to do the work that needs to be done. Unfortunately, your investors don't have a robust growth portfolio like most venture capitalists, angel investors, or other early stage funding sources. They made one investment—you and your team—and they expect a return.

Your investors are also terribly impatient. They expect a quick and sizable return on their investment because every quarter, they must justify their investment to the board, market analysts, and actual investors and shareholders who have the power to make your investors very uncomfortable, unhappy, and even unemployed. Assuming everyone prefers to stay comfortable, happy, and employed, you must produce results.

First, though, you need to define them.

Realistic Results

You defined the growth gap, so you know what your investors want. You know that achieving that result takes time, and you can't go from nothing to $250 million in one giant step. It takes lots of steps to achieve your ultimate goal.

Steps that can produce results this year.

Hope produced results in year 1 when she "turned on the lights" by compiling MaXperience's innovation portfolio and comparing it to the company's growth gap in three months. Faith's work on quick wins produced results in year 2, but she had to do something Hope didn't. She had to solve the problem of finding short-term results her team could deliver without distracting them and delaying the delivery of longer-term goals.

That's a problem that needs some love.

To love a problem, you must learn about it.

To learn about it, you must talk to people.

The beginning of a new year is the perfect time to talk to your stakeholder-investors. It's a perfectly reasonable time to update them on your progress and reassure them that your eye remains on the prize—filling the growth gap. Then, ever so casually, you ask for their thoughts on what you shared. How would they characterize your progress? What do they think of your priorities? What is their definition of success for this year? You're not asking for a decision from them, and you're not committing. You're just curious.

Then offer examples of results you can deliver to gauge the overlap with the results they need. Suggest things that can be seen and measured, activity metrics like website visits or consumer feedback on prototypes, that are important but not mission critical to the person you're talking to, and that you have more than an 80 percent chance of being able to deliver. For Faith, that included a portfolio of fewer higher-impact projects, improvements in employee satisfaction, and a tangible change to the onboarding process.

Once you understand what your stakeholders need and want to see and their openness to the results you suggested, reevaluate your portfolio. Look for ways to produce quick wins without adding work to your team's already full plate, even if it means taking something off the plate. When everything is a priority, nothing is a priority.

Priorities

Speaking of priorities, most organizations find themselves in the same situation as Faith—too many ideas, suggestions, pet projects, and initiatives already in progress. Sorting through them can be difficult and prioritizing them can be even more challenging. The goal of developing a completely objective turnkey prioritization tool is noble but unrealistic. There are too many unknowns, and hard-earned intuition is essential in learning environments. Instead, create a discussion tool that minimizes subjectivity and encourages informed debate.

Faith created an innovation playground that made prioritization simpler and slightly less controversial by looking at projects from multiple angles. It also went beyond a binary yes/no assessment of the project's performance across multiple parameters to a range from attractive (the organization would eagerly pursue), through

Innovation thrives within **constraints.**

discussable, to out of bounds (the organization would never consider something like it).

The innovation playground is a simple table with four columns and any number of rows. The leftmost column lists the parameters used to evaluate projects, while the next columns are titled in play (or desirable), in bounds (or discussable), and out of bounds (or off limits). Each row represents an attribute or metric used to assess the attractiveness of an opportunity area or solution and the criteria it must meet to be in play, in bounds, or out of bounds. Below is an example of Faith's innovation playground.

Build Your Playground

Creating an innovation playground is collaborative and iterative because everyone must agree with the parameters and criteria. If decision-makers and stakeholders don't agree with the basic definitions, they'll never agree with the resulting assessment, and conversations will go in circles. Garbage in, garbage out, so don't rush the process. Faith spent two months developing and socializing her innovation playground and realized almost immediate results.

Start by brainstorming a long list of potential parameters. Then look for the ten or so that ultimately determine whether something is worth investment. Ideally, the parameters are the same at each stage of the process, and only the definitions of in play, in bounds, and out of bounds change. This consistency helps when comparing projects across multiple stages, but it's okay if you need to add or remove a few parameters for specific stages. Determining parameters is often the most challenging and time-consuming step. To avoid being overwhelmed, start with the stage where you have the most projects and determine those dimensions first.

Once you have a short list of parameters, brainstorm definitions for in play, in bounds, and out of bounds for each parameter. The previous step may have taken the most time, but this step sparks

DIMENSIONS	IN PLAY (DESIRABLE)	IN BOUNDS (DISCUSSABLE)	OUT OF BOUNDS (OFF LIMITS)
Strategic Fit	Develop new financial products	Expand existing financial services	Anything that doesn't align with our core financial services
Customer Benefit	Helps customers manage wealth and investments	Improves customer financial literacy	Products that do not provide clear financial benefits to customers
Full Launch Date	2 years from today	3 years from today	4+ years from today
Year 1 Revenue	$10M+	$2M–$9.99M	Less than $2M
5-Year Cumulative Revenue	$100M+	$20M–$99.99M	Less than $20M
Geographic Markets	US and EU	Existing markets	Markets where we do not currently do business
Target Customers (Who pays?)	Institutional investors High-net-worth individuals Retail customers	Small and medium-sized enterprises	Unbanked populations

Target Financial Advisors (Who uses?)	Wealth managers Financial planners Investment advisors	Insurance agents Loan officers	Nonfinancial professionals
Target Financial Applications	Wealth management Investment advisory Retirement planning	Insurance products Loan products	Noncore financial services
Registration Required	SEC (US) FCA (UK)	State-level financial regulations	No regulatory oversight
Capabilities Required	Leverage all existing capabilities, especially: • Risk management • Data analytics • In-house development of new products	Partner to access required capabilities Hire individuals with required capabilities	M&A to access required capabilities

the most debate because defining what makes something attractive, interesting, and worthy of discussion is subjective. The debate, however, won't be what you think. There is rarely a debate about what the definitions should be; it's usually whether there should be definitions at all.

People hesitate to define what makes something more or less attractive, fearing that setting criteria constrains innovation. It does, and that's awesome! Innovation thrives within constraints because constraints demand creativity and drive focus and efficiency. Innovation without constraints is wasteful chaos, so set the constraints yourself. Define what is out of bounds for every single dimension. When defining what is in play (attractive), make sure the attributes and metrics are reasonable and tied to the overall goals of the innovation team, including the growth gap you defined in year 1. Everything else is in bounds for now.

Test Your Playground

When you have a first draft, apply the playground to three projects: one that should be deprioritized (i.e., out of bounds), one that should be a priority (in play), and one in which the fit isn't yet obvious. Assess each project against each dimension by assigning a score of 3 for in play, 2 for in bounds, and 1 for out of bounds and plotting each score on a spider or radar chart. Look at the chart. Is the area outlined by the project you should work on larger than the area for the other two projects? Is the area outlined by the project that wasn't a fit smaller? It's okay if some dimensions score a 1. What matters is the overall area outlined and the intent to use this as a tool to raise and focus discussion rather than churn out answers. (That's why you don't want to total the scores and approve anything with a score over X and cut anything with a score lower than Y.) Iterate the dimensions, attributes, and metrics until you get charts that look like what you expect based on your understanding of the project and the business.

Share Your Playground

For the playground to prompt the intended discussions and decisions, people need to understand what it is and isn't, how it will and won't be used, and feel like it reflects their perspective. Therefore, it's important to share a draft of the innovation playground and ask for feedback before you use it. Explain it to your team, peers, and key stakeholders. Let them play with it and apply it to their pet projects. Then ask for feedback. Keep revising and socializing until everyone is on board with the parameters and definitions.

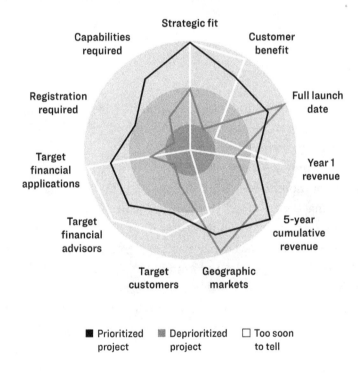

Adapted from Scott D. Anthony, Mark W. Johnson, Joseph V. Sinfield, and Elizabeth J. Altman, *The Innovator's Guide to Growth: Putting Disruptive Innovation to Work* (Harvard Business Press, 2008).

Use Your Playground Often and Consistently

Organizations tend to either reject this tool for fear that they'll lose the freedom and flexibility "required" to be innovative and "respond to rapidly changing environments," *or* they love it to death by immediately applying it to everything, even to the most minor feature on the smallest continuous innovation project. Both reactions are dangerous. So, go slow. Use it on projects within a specific phase of your innovation process or that are being worked on by one particular team. People usually need about six months of using it to experience the benefits. When that happens, the playground becomes a very fun place to be.

Decisions

You have a discussion tool and some priorities identified. None of that matters if you don't do your job. Your job is to make decisions.

A shocking number of executives don't.

Instead, they delay by asking for more data, more people to weigh in, or more time. It's not that they don't want to make decisions. It's that they're afraid they'll make the wrong ones, and if they do, they'll be punished by their bosses. It's critical that we remember, and remind others who may also have forgotten, that decisions aren't final, unchangeable, and immutable. A decision is a choice made based on the data available at that moment. It can and should be questioned when more information is available, and it can and should be changed if underlying hypotheses are not true.

Who Decides?

As an innovation leader, you generally make three types of decisions:

1 When to grow (or shrink) the team
2 When to invest and how much to invest
3 Whether to advance, pivot, or kill a project

Big decisions like multimillion-dollar investments or firing a team member require lots of information, discussion, and debate. Small decisions like whether to use yak hair or human hair for a product demo (we chose yak) or the type of cookie to order for a happy hour don't require much, if any, information, discussion, or debate.

Small decisions don't require you. Big ones do. Sometimes it's hard for executives to tell the difference, and they lean too far to one side or another, either abdicating all responsibility and claiming they are empowering their team or micromanaging every decision, even if it means oatmeal raisin cookies at the happy hour.

If you ever debate whether a decision requires your involvement, here's a handy rule of thumb. Calculate your salary per hour, then estimate the hours of reading, thinking, discussing, meeting, and other activities required to make the decision. Multiply the number of hours required to make the decision by your hourly salary to get the time cost of making the decision. Now look at the financial impact of the decision: the amount of money the organization stands to gain or lose, earn or spend as a result of the decision. If the cost of your time to make the decision exceeds the financial impact of the decision, delegate.*

Once you determine which decisions you need to make, you can move on to determining who makes all the other decisions. Start by determining if a decision can be made by one person or a small group of people or if it requires input from a wide variety of people outside your immediate organization. It's tempting to institute

---

* Like all rules of thumb, it's not perfect, and it doesn't apply in every scenario. It can also be depressing. Years ago, I was told to itemize my mobile phone bill before I expensed it, and I pitched a fit, claiming that my time was more valuable than the financial impact of the bill. In a fit of self-righteous indignation, convinced I was about to prove my point, I calculated my salary per minute. Turns out my time was a lot less valuable than I thought and itemizing the bill was indeed a valuable use of it.

a resource accountability matrix like RACI or RASCI at this point, but be wary of doing so if it's not already an embedded part of your team's culture. Innovation requires flexibility and a "we're all in this together" mindset. In companies where this approach or mindset isn't the norm, I've seen RACIs become weaponized and used to avoid helping out or to justify placing blame. Instead, establish norms and expectations with your team that outline generally who owns what and specifically that multiple voices need to be heard.

How to Decide

There are two keys to making decisions fearlessly: matching the decision to be made with the available information and following a transparent and consistent process.

The main reason most executives don't make decisions is that they want enough data to ensure that the ultimate goal—whether it's annual revenue of $250 million, market leadership, global expansion, or FDA approval—happens. It's the business equivalent of basing your decision on having a child on the availability of data proving they'll be a professional softball player. The data doesn't exist.

When you don't have a lot of data, don't make big decisions. Just like you don't have a child because you saw a cute kid in the park that one time, don't give an employee with a cool idea but no track record of building a business a blank check. As you gather more data, your confidence increases, and bigger decisions are warranted. But remember no matter how much data you collect, there's no guarantee that the ultimate goal is achieved.

That's why transparency and consistency are also essential in your decision-making process.

One of the most consistent elements of human behavior I've witnessed is our ability to fill in knowledge gaps with the worst-case scenario. I am constantly impressed by the dark creativity most people demonstrate when trying to explain how and why a decision was made. I'm also impressed that the stories are never true.

When you don't have a lot of data, **don't make big decisions.**

Focus your team's and your colleagues' creativity on more positive topics by being uncomfortable, transparent, and relentlessly consistent in how you make decisions. When you realize a decision needs to be made, outline how you will make it. If the criteria change, proactively communicate the change. When the decision is made, be sure that it was made according to the criteria listed. If it wasn't, explain why. If it was, explain how each criterion was used and led to the decision made. For some decisions, the innovation playground enables transparency because you've already done the hard work of defining criteria, but there are other decisions that the innovation playground doesn't speak to. Being transparent with those decisions is tougher and just as important.

Consistent transparency is also essential. If you explain some decisions but not others, the stories that fill the gaps tend to go from dark to sinister. Every decision needs an explanation. Cancel a project after two years of development? Explain it. Decide to pursue an idea through a partnership versus building the product in-house? Explain it. Order a salad instead of your usual turkey sandwich? Explain it.

When to Decide

Like figuring out which decisions to make, determining when to make decisions isn't as easy as it seems. Sometimes, decision points are obvious because you know the lead time required or when critical data will be available. But usually it's the little decisions you make between the obvious decision points that determine the fate of the project and the effectiveness of your team.

Scheduled meetings must happen frequently enough that the team gets the guidance they need and executives maintain confidence that progress is happening. If meetings are too frequent, the team spends more time preparing (no matter how often you tell them not to) than working on projects. If meetings aren't frequent enough, the team could go down a path that is unattractive or even problematic for critical stakeholders, wasting precious time and budget.

Figuring out what works takes time and experimentation, so I recommend the 80/20 rule—the team should spend 80 percent of their time between meetings working on innovation and 20 percent preparing for formal updates. Meeting monthly means about 3.5 weeks working on innovation and three days preparing for a meeting. If your team spends a week or more preparing for a meeting, you must either manage your peers' expectations regarding what they'll get in update meetings or schedule meetings every two to three months to allow 1.5 to 2.5 weeks to prepare for meetings.

As lovely as it would be if life and innovation operated on your schedule, that doesn't often happen. Expect the unexpected and ill timed. I've seen three different approaches work:

- **Scheduled stand-ups:** If you live and die by your calendar, travel frequently, or juggle a massive scope of work, schedule twice-weekly ten- to fifteen-minute stand-ups with the team that can be attended in-person or by phone. These meetings signify your commitment to the team, so don't change or cancel them. They also ensure you won't be surprised by something days or weeks after it occurs.

- **Twenty-four-hour response policy:** If you work in a hybrid setting, want time to think things over before making decisions, or are great at managing your time, promise to respond to all calls, emails, and texts within twenty-four hours. This sets the team's expectation for when they receive an answer, buys you time to manage and think while juggling multiple other priorities, and ensures that you aren't a bottleneck to the team's progress.

- **Open-door policy:** If your schedule is flexible, you're located with the team, and you don't mind interruptions, an open-door policy facilitates immediate discussion and resolution of issues.

These approaches have pros and cons, so choosing one you can stick to is the most critical factor. Suppose you constantly change or cancel scheduled stand-ups, take days or weeks to respond to emails and calls, or adopt an open-door policy but are inaccessible due to meetings and travel. In that case, your actions tell the team that the issue isn't important. After all, "I don't have time" means "It's not a priority."

TL;DR Year 2 Architecture

Ideas are a dime a dozen. Decisions are priceless.

Produce results that grab people's attention, demonstrate change, and generate financial results.

- Ask your stakeholders about the changes they're experiencing and that they hope to see.
- Deliver quick wins that create value. They won't be glamorous, but they will give you evidence of progress.

Define your priorities because if everything is a priority, nothing is a priority.

- Define your portfolio by documenting what your team is working on and where the projects are in the process.
- Establish your innovation playground by defining what makes a project in play, in bounds, or out of bounds.
- Prioritize your portfolio by comparing each project to the playground and your available resources. Invest in the projects that fit the playground and give you the biggest bang for your buck. Cut everything else.

Decide how to decide so your team can quickly and confidently move forward.

- Decide who decides. Big money decisions with big implications require you. Small decisions don't. But they do require someone, so be clear about who that is.
- Be transparent about what you need to make a decision, recognizing you'll never have all the data you want.
- Communicate early and often the decisions made and how you decided.

Know Your Decision-Making Models

RESPONSIBILITY ASSIGNMENT TOOLS like RACI, RASCI, and PACE are proven models for determining decision-making responsibility. They're great when a big team is working on a big project facing more knowns than unknowns. They're not great for innovation because, as my clients and I have discovered, they're too complex and complicated for innovation projects run by small teams requiring rapid decisions. Instead, we use a 4+ decision-making model.

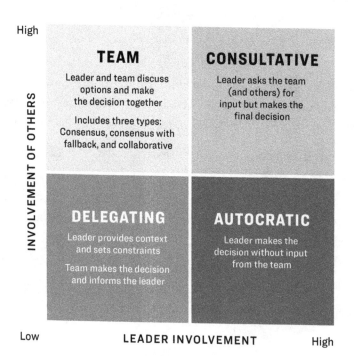

High

TEAM

Leader and team discuss options and make the decision together

Includes three types: Consensus, consensus with fallback, and collaborative

CONSULTATIVE

Leader asks the team (and others) for input but makes the final decision

INVOLVEMENT OF OTHERS

DELEGATING

Leader provides context and sets constraints

Team makes the decision and informs the leader

AUTOCRATIC

Leader makes the decision without input from the team

Low   LEADER INVOLVEMENT   High

At the start of a project, we agree on who the one and only leader is, then brainstorm all the significant decisions we anticipate making and decide which box in the model they fall into. For decisions that fall into the team decision box, we then discuss and agree on whether we use consensus (unanimous agreement is required to move forward), consensus with fallback (if consensus can't be reached by a given date, the leader decides), or collaborative (vote on a decision as agree, agree with reservations, abstain and publicly support, or block and actively participate in resolving the block). The discussion sounds quite pedantic when written out, but it typically moves quickly, with most of the time spent debating who the one and only leader is.

Here's an example of the tool in use.

A team was at a critical point in a project where foundational research and initial exploration were wrapping up. They were in the midst of ideation, and prototype development was about to begin. Working together, we realized that we needed guardrails to continue working from ideation into prototyping because many of the ideas we came up with weren't consistent with the company's product development and launch road map.

When the team asked executives for guidance, the executives pushed back, expressing their belief that because the team was closer to the user, the team was best suited to make decisions. The team left the meeting frustrated. Lots of activity followed, but there was no meaningful progress. In meetings, the team would bring ideas to the executive team for feedback and receive lots of questions and requests for more examples or data, actions that executives intended as helpful training to teach the team how to think but which were interpreted as doubt or disagreement and a demand to do more work.

As the project stalled, the project leader called a meeting to address the dispute head-on and dig into the root causes of the slowdown. We presented the 4+ decision-making model, and the team reflected that they were uncomfortable with executives' stated desire to delegate decisions. In response, executives shared that they were frustrated by what they perceived as the team's desire for autocratic decision-making, in which executives told the teams precisely what to do. With a model to use as a common reference point, everyone felt comfortable sharing their intent and perceptions, and the team could work together to find a working solution.

Of course, the working solution was that most decisions would use a team decision-making model. This surfaced a new set of challenges rooted in the differing intent and perception of executive questions and requests in response to team ideas and proposals.

Initially, the team gravitated toward a consensus model until the project manager pointed out that there was a project plan with key milestones, and a consensus approach put those deadlines at risk. After a few more minutes of discussion, the team agreed on a collaborative approach for most decisions in the future.

A few weeks later, this approach was tested when the team recommended a course of action that required critical trade-offs in the features and functions of the proposed solution. As usual, the executives asked many questions and suggested speaking to dozens more people, all things that would have delayed or even derailed the team in the past. However, no one cast a block vote when it came time to vote. Everyone agreed with the recommendation or approved with reservations and set up offline conversations to discuss further.

Everyone left the meeting confident that they had been heard and understood the next steps.

10

Culture
Share, Invite, and Expand

IN YEAR 1, you protected your innovation team by building walls around them to protect them from the mindsets and processes that drive the core business and put the brakes on change. After all, your team and their work were precious and fragile, and like a newborn, they needed to be protected and incubated.

It's year 2, and your team isn't a fragile newborn anymore. It's time to start breaking down those walls because "when one looks at innovation in nature and in culture," Steven Johnson wrote in *Where Good Ideas Come From*, "environments that build walls around good ideas tend to be less innovative in the long run than more open-ended environments."

Share Your Stories

As humans, we're hardwired to share and remember stories. Through stories, we discover and communicate our personal and professional identities, navigate the world around us, share ideas across cultural and organizational boundaries, and find purpose in what we do.

Here's the origin story of a beloved and wildly successful innovation:

In the process of developing an adhesive strong enough to be used in aircraft construction, a research chemist discovered that a copolymer composed of 95 to 99 percent acrylate monomer and 1 to 5 percent of a mixture containing iconic monomers and maleic anhydride produced an adhesive that could be dispersed as an aerosol spray. The resulting microspheres, measuring 50 to 75 µm, flatten when pressed against a surface, providing moderate sheer strength due to an increase in van der Waals forces while maintaining low peel strength.

Sound familiar? If not, what about this version?

Frustrated by bookmarks constantly falling out his hymnal, a 3M research scientist wondered if there was a better way to mark his place in the book without damaging the pages. Little did he know that just down the hall, one of his colleagues had spent the last six years nurturing just such a solution.

Both of those stories are about 3M's Post-it Note, but you probably only recognized the second story. The stories people remember are either relatable or so fantastic that they spark our imaginations. The second Post-it story sticks (sorry, I couldn't resist) and spreads because we know what it's like to lose our place in a book because too many of the pages are dog-eared or a bookmark fluttered to the floor. We remember and retell a story because we identify with the people in the story, share their frustrations, and yearn for a better solution.

Over the past year, you and your team turned experiences into stories. Tales of things gone right or wrong, of unexpected consequences, and inconsequential moments. Some of the stories are specific to your team and that moment, but some deserve a wider audience. The first step in breaking down the walls that once protected your team and spreading your culture of innovation is expanding out and sharing your stories.

When you talk to your stakeholders, tell them stories about your team's hard work that led to exceptional insights and are now fueling the creation of new offerings or business models destined to drive exponential growth. Encourage your team to share stories with their colleagues about their work in the trenches, the lessons that could only be learned through experience, and the exhilaration of doing things they never imagined possible.

Faith did this consistently. She invited quick wins teams to share updates at leadership meetings, which developed their storytelling skills, rather than presenting the teams' work herself. She shared her in-progress and "more right than wrong" versions of the innovation playground with eventual users and asked them to provide input. She encouraged people throughout the team to share both good and bad stories of attending fewer meetings so others could understand the impact and make better-informed decisions.

Faith consistently sparked and encouraged conversations because she knew that when your stakeholders and colleagues hear your innovation stories early and often, they're more likely to stay engaged and interested in your work and to repeat and retell your stories to people within their organizations. This plants the seed of the innovation culture you hope to spread. Stories nurture those seeds better than data ever can.

Invite People In

Lunch together around the too small conference room table. Friday happy hours. Winter holiday parties. Summer family outings. In addition to stories, you and your team built habits and traditions. These rituals, as academics call them, are incredibly important for your team because they embody your values and reinforce your culture. Like stories, some should stay exclusive to your team, but others are opportunities to spread your culture by inviting people in.

When I was on the Swiffer team, every day six of us, representing three different new product teams, ate lunch around a table for four people. This time was sacred and fiercely exclusive because it gave us the time and freedom to commiserate and laugh about our shared experiences of creating something new in an organization that fiercely defended the status quo. Happy hours, though, were a different story. Every Friday, we'd walk the halls of the ninth floor to rally the rest of our brand colleagues to join us at the Rock Bottom Brewery a few blocks away. It was the end of the week, and we all needed time to relax, enjoy ourselves, and let off some steam.

Winter holiday parties were another affair exclusive to the new business development team but, unlike our lunches, included our teammates in every function. Summer outings to Kings Island, an amusement park just north of Cincinnati, were a P&G tradition. Every employee and their family were invited to the park for a day, giving us time to reconnect with old colleagues, meet new people, and enjoy time with friends and family.

Events and traditions form and evolve naturally, so they are often the most authentic and stickiest cultural tool. As a leader, you don't need to be involved in each one. You shouldn't be. Instead, keep an eye on them to ensure they embody the culture you intend to create. If they don't, talk to one or more members of your team to understand how they took shape and figure out how to reshape them to align with the team's desired culture and share values. If they embody your desired culture, encourage the team to open up a bit and invite people in. The best way to expand your culture is to let others experience it and spread the message for you.

One word of caution: everyone can be an innovator, but not everyone wants to be, and not everyone needs to be. Remember what I told

Everyone can
be an innovator,
but not everyone
wants to be,
**and not everyone
needs to be.**

you in "Know Your Innovators. Celebrate Your Operators." Some people genuinely like mastering a process or skill or becoming an expert in a topic. They don't see the need to jump to the next big thing, chase after a new shiny object, or follow the latest fad when there is so much more to be discovered and done where they currently work.

Innovators tend to see these people as old-fashioned sticks-in-the-mud hellbent on suffocating innovation by evangelizing the ideology of "If it ain't broke, don't fix it." While I understand the kneejerk, eye-rolling, instinctive reaction, these people are *awesome*!

You and your organization *need* these people because they keep you in business during the years before your innovations launch and earn revenue. These people keep you competitive, providing improved customer offerings and fending off competitors. Their hard work keeps the lights on and the paychecks from bouncing. Love these people. Thank them for their hard work and patience. Ask for their advice and input.

Then leave them alone.

They don't want to play your innovation games.

Don't make them.

Expand Your Influence

Sharing your stories and inviting people into your traditions and events allow people curious about what this innovation stuff is to experience the culture you're building. You give them the opportunity to learn what you're doing and why. They learn how you're doing your work and can explore how to use your tools and frameworks in their daily work.

At this point, you'll sense that demand for these experiences is high, and you'll be tempted to take a wrecking ball to the protective walls around your team and invite the masses in. Don't. If you do anything more than take the walls down brick by brick, you will be loved to death—a phenomenon that occurs when everyone interested in innovation swarms the team, consuming so much of the team's time that they no longer have any left to do their work. It's the business equivalent of being trampled to death by puppies.

Instead, start small.

Find a team or two that benefits from a new approach and teach them about discovery tools like Jobs to Be Done, empathy interviews, ethnography, and observational research. Find an initiative struggling to break out of traditional thinking and facilitate an ideation session. Host a lunch-and-learn to share new insights or a show-and-tell to let people experience and give feedback on rough prototypes.

As you engage small pockets of interested people in innovation, spend time teaching them and help them understand what innovation is and isn't. (I guarantee they all have their own definitions, and none match yours.) Explain the growth gap that innovation needs to deliver. Encourage them to be creative and curious in their daily work, then share stories of what that looks like and how to do it well.

Faith started small so that she improved her team's odds of success when she went big in year 3. She sent two of her direct reports out into the organization to work with a handful of operations and innovation teams to test messages, stories, and tools and learn what resonated. She collected feedback on what worked and what didn't in the core business, and she experienced the practical ways in which innovation and operations differ and where each side could be improved by the other. She also built an army of storytellers, advocates, and champions, giving leaders at all levels of the organization the raw materials they needed to craft their own stories; be curious, courageous, and creative leaders; and support innovation when, in year 3, she would go big with events like hackathons and shark tanks, wow everyone with demo days, and release a library full of tools, templates, and training.

Patience is not a trait typically associated with innovators, but you need to practice it. Time and again, I've seen innovation leaders go too big too fast and flame out. They struggle to maintain momentum, support their teams, deliver results, and inspire the change the rest of the organization expects.

You're making progress, and while it may feel small, it is essential to achieving your ultimate goals.

TL;DR Year 2 Culture

A leader without followers is a lonely person out for a walk. As you attract followers, you expand culture.

Share your stories so that people connect to and spread your successes.

- Make the stories relatable, so people can envision themselves as main characters and, one day, the hero.
- Tell stories about experiments that went wrong or unexpected insights and what you did next that led to learning or success.
- Encourage people to spread your stories or even adopt them as their own.

Invite in aspiring innovators.

- Include people in your team's rituals and traditions. Invite them to team happy hours or grab lunch or coffee together.
- Teach people what innovation means at your company and how it's done.
- Create contained moments for people to be creative.
- Thank the operators for the value they create.

Help the organization learn how to be more curious, creative, and committed.

- Compliment people when they follow your lead and demonstrate curiosity, courage, and commitment.
- Enroll like-minded peers to help you spread the culture of innovation throughout your organization.
- Plan how to spread the message through small-person activities, big-group events, and everything in between.

YEAR THREE

11

Victor

THE PAST two years were a slow, steady, and often frustrating march to prove that Rena & Holmes (R&H), a 125-year-old company, could innovate. Victor loved every minute of it.

He'd always been drawn to roles everyone else saw as thankless, unglamorous, or impossible but that he knew gave him the freedom to challenge the status quo, be creative, and have an outsized impact. That's why he left a successful sales career to start over in an entry-level marketing role. It's why he was happy to work in the smallest business unit, the one that didn't really make any sense within a company famous for its cleaning products. It's why he jumped at the chance to lead an innovation team, even though it meant giving up his P&L responsibilities.

But as year 3 started, he felt his fun and freedom slipping away despite evidence that the company's identity and operations were changing because of the work he'd led in years 1 and 2.

Year 1

Rena & Holmes was in the midst of a reorganization designed to simplify operations and accelerate decision-making. Executives throughout the company were waking up to the fact that new competitors were gaining market share and that change was needed to maintain the reputational, performance, and price premiums they had always enjoyed.

As part of shaking off its sleepy complacency, the CEO mandated the creation of innovation teams within each of the company's business units. Handpicked executives assumed control of each team, and each inherited a project that seemed promising from a technical standpoint but had languished and even failed in test markets. "You have a year to turn this around," the CEO told each executive. "Tell me what you need."

The project Victor inherited began two years prior when the business unit's vice president realized he could not deliver his P&L goals by relying solely on incremental innovation. However, the product's test market sales proved that consumers wouldn't buy something just because it's technologically interesting.

When it launched into the test market, FreshAyre targeted smokers and promised to eliminate the smell of cigarette smoke from their clothes and home. As was typical for the company, the advertising spoke to the functional benefit of using the product and illustrated how its chemistry uniquely solved it. For six months, the product sat on store shelves, collecting dust despite heavy advertising and couponing.

Then Victor arrived.

Ignoring advice from more senior executives to cut his losses, pull the product, and direct scarce resources toward something new, Victor doubled down. He refused to end the test before understanding why the product failed. He was confident that the learnings would help the company avoid future failures and even trigger a turnaround for this product.

He instructed his team to forget about the usual business metrics. They were no longer concerned with revenue, units sold, or profit margins. They were to stay myopically focused on finding the root cause of the product's failure and running experiments to turn it around.

As for the process, paperwork, and bureaucracy that the company hadn't yet shaken off? Victor assured the team he would handle it. If people started asking questions, refusing to help, or erecting barriers, Victor would talk to them. The team's job was to learn. Victor's was to create the environment that enabled that to happen.

The team practically lived in the test market. They filled their days with research: talking to consumers in stores, visiting people in their homes to watch them use the product, and meeting with store managers and buyers to solicit their advice and input. At night, the team gathered to share insights and brainstorm new ideas. Every three to four months, they changed the product's strategy and positioning, noting what worked and what didn't.

Meanwhile, Victor bounced between the test market and headquarters. When he was with the team, he rolled up his sleeves and worked alongside them as peers, stocking shelves, asking questions, and sharing ideas. At headquarters, he constantly wandered the halls, sharing stories and updates with stakeholders and senior executives, showing them data, and inviting them to visit the test market.

Even when something went wrong or the data wasn't good, Victor shared it. He put it in context, explained what was learned, and how it informed decisions about what to do next. He celebrated it as evidence of the team's creativity and courage, the mindsets that the reorganization hoped to embed.

People noticed. Executives paid more attention to the product. Peers asked questions about what he was doing and why. Process owners became prickly, raising concerns about legal, financial, and operational risks. And just as he'd promised, Victor handled it. His days were filled with conversations, one-on-ones, coffee chats, and "accidental" run-ins in the hallway. He listened to opinions and acknowledged concerns. He asked who else he should talk to who may also have thoughts and concerns and then had conversations with them. And he always, always, always explained the why behind his decisions and actions.

Twelve months after they started, Victor's team found the root cause of the failure: they had followed the company's playbook by identifying a very specific target segment and assuming that logic and chemistry were sufficient to surface a problem and convince their target to pay money and change behavior to solve it. Doing the opposite would be their path to success.

Year 2

The turnaround began in earnest.

Marketing shifted focus from cigarette smokers who *should* want to eliminate the smell of smoke from their clothes to consumers who believed a scent-free home was a clean home and were frustrated that their only options for eliminating odors were perfume-heavy sprays, candles, and air fresheners. Messaging shifted from a focus on FreshAyre's unique chemistry to promising clean scent-free air and peace of mind that guests would never smell last night's dinner, the dog's frolic in the rain, or the family's yet-to-be-done laundry. Advertising shifted from traditional media to in-store demos, public relations events, and product partnerships so people could experience FreshAyre's benefits. Even the sales channels expanded to include nontraditional outlets like home improvement stores, car dealerships, and vacation rentals.

Inside R&H, the lines between different functions' responsibilities that had blurred in year 1 dissolved at the start of year 2. It was no longer R&D's job to make the product, marketing's job to sell it, and supply chain's job to deliver it. They were all in this together—working together as equals, sharing ideas, and respecting each other's areas of expertise.

Doing the opposite would be their **path to success.**

People noticed. Executives sought Victor out, wanting the latest updates and stories. Peers asked for advice on inspiring their teams to work as creatively and efficiently as his. Process owners were still prickly, but a few realized that this new way of working was about to become the norm and started to adapt and redesign processes to support it.

But the turnaround wasn't the only thing on Victor's mind.

Based on the success of his first year, his portfolio expanded from one project to six, all in different phases of development and all with different challenges. His team grew, too, but Victor took the same approach—he battled the bureaucracy so his teams could focus on learning.

At the end of year 2, Victor's original team launched FreshAyre in North America and prepared to launch it in Europe and Asia. Another team was turning around FresaWash, another failed product, and two teams were preparing to pilot their products—ClnFlr, a floor cleaner, and Renseri, a new laundry product for hard-to-clean clothes.

Even without revenue, Victor's results were obvious and his success unquestioned.

He was promoted to general manager and vice president.

With so much success and a swanky new title, Victor hoped year 3 would be easy.

Year 3

As the new year dawned, Victor realized nothing would be easy.

Employee satisfaction, engagement, and retention were at all-time highs because people throughout the organization were experiencing fun and freedom they had never imagined. Managers no longer relied on a command-and-control approach, demanding to know every detail and approve every decision. Instead, they empowered their teams, defining which decisions they had to make and which could be made by their direct reports. Some managers even gave each team member a small "no strings attached" budget to explore new ideas and run experiments. Yet the majority of the organization continued to struggle with the changes and shifts required to keep up with innovators within and beyond its walls.

The organization's famously insular culture was opening up. Partnerships with other companies, universities, and even entrepreneurs were established. Teams were encouraged to spend time outside the office, wandering through stores and neighborhoods in search of inspiration and new ideas. Unfortunately, R&H's famously conservative culture put the brakes on the process of finding ideas, creating partnerships, and incubating businesses, as anything outside standard operating procedure was flagged, debated, and often denied.

Victor's teams operated like well-oiled machines, had access to the resources they needed, and had a process in place that was purpose-built to move fast and navigate uncertainty, but his portfolio was producing mixed results. ClnFlr was going well and exceeding all expectations in the test markets. Renseri was doing okay in its pilot, but the team faced disinformation campaigns and bad publicity from industry groups and struggled with how to respond. Consumers loved FresaWash, but retailers wouldn't shelve it in the right category, so sales were abysmal. TeniSuds, a shoe cleaner, struggled to find product-market fit. LavoLux, an appliance that allowed people to dry-clean their clothes at home, was being developed in partnership with another company, and the two were locked in an endless loop of legal negotiations about intellectual property ownership and decision-making rights.

He had the C-suite's support and his peers' trust, and revenue from FreshAyre was on track to deliver double its forecasted revenue, but all of the fun and freedom Victor had enjoyed in his first two years were gone. He felt like an operator now, responsible for building and launching a steady stream of hundred-million-dollar projects, as if innovation was an assembly line capable of churning out consistent and repeatable results despite high ambiguity, uncertainty, and risk.

He wanted fun and freedom. Instead, he faced the first real threat to his team's existence.

The Challenge

Even though the reorg had gone well, business results weren't coming in as expected. Revenue was down, and the company was at risk of missing earnings. Executives were confident this was a temporary blip, and the business would bounce back. But confidence doesn't convert to cash, so budgets across the organization were slashed and funds funneled to the biggest brands.

Victor knew his team wouldn't be immune to the cuts for long, despite the potential revenue each project represented. So, he prepared for the inevitable. He asked his team what activities they could quickly start and stop. What can we cut without significantly impacting our progress? What activities, if stopped, compromise the viability of the business?

He explained to his bosses that innovation isn't something that can be turned on or off like a faucet. You can't stop a project and then pick it back up months or years later, right where you left off. Once you lose momentum, things move backward. Consumers forget about you, retailers doubt you, and team members pursue other opportunities.

The inevitable came.

But not in the way Victor expected.

Once you lose momentum, **things move backward.**

The Meeting

"We can't launch based on this data."

Victor's head whipped to his left. He couldn't believe what he heard. ClnFlr's team had just presented their recommendation to launch the product and forecasted $300 million in year 1 revenue. It would be the company's biggest launch ever, exceeding the $200 million FreshAyre generated.

But despite outstanding test market sales and a conservative revenue forecast, the CEO homed in on one specific piece of data.

For the past thirty years, every product the company launched had been run through a simulation to ensure that test market data was nationally representative. Brand teams fed information about sales distribution, marketing spending, and anticipated competitive responses into a black box, and the black box spit out its prediction for the product's year 1 revenue and market share.

In thirty years, the black box simulation had never been wrong.

It had also never been used on a category-defining new product.

When the team received the results, they panicked. The market simulation results weren't just bad. They were historically bad. They predicted the launch would be the third worst in the industry's history.

When Victor saw the results, he sighed. He knew this was coming. He had fought for months to avoid using this simulation because its methodology was designed to make predictions based on perfectly analogous products. Markets that don't exist can't be measured, let alone forecasted, he explained. He lost the battle. He sure as hell wasn't going to lose the war.

With the refusal to launch ringing in his ears, Victor slammed his palms on the table and rose from his seat. He only made it halfway to standing before he felt a gentle touch on his arm. Turning to his right, he saw the COO give a slight nod.

"I don't believe the data," the COO huffed. "I went to the test market. I saw the empty shelves because the product sold out. I listened to people talk about how much they love this product and how it's changed their lives. There's something wrong with the data. This needs to launch."

The debate began. The beloved and well-respected CEO calmly explained that such a risk was too great to take, given the current environment. The embattled COO repeated the same argument about the simulation's methodology flaws that Victor had made to him months before.

Back and forth they went. Flipping through pages in the presentation, citing data, and referencing past decisions. They seemed destined to stalemate or, worse, for the CEO to win because he outranked the COO.

"If it fails, fire me."

Silence. Every head turned slowly to look at Victor.

"If it fails, fire me," he repeated. "I believe in my team and this product. Like the COO, I've seen how people respond to it in the real world, and I don't believe the black box. Give us a chance, and if I'm wrong, fire me."

Five Months Later

The auditorium was packed with five thousand people—the entire North American sales team for R&H. "The Final Countdown," which had been blasting on the speakers, faded down and the lights on the stage rose. Victor saw his cue and walked to the podium.

Months ago, he put his job, career, and reputation on the line to get ClnFlr launched. Today was the first step in that process. How the sales force reacted to the presentation would be the first indication of whether or not he would have a job this time next year.

As he wrapped up his presentation, the applause was deafening. The famously skeptical sales force was on its feet, eager to get its hands on the new product and start selling it. It was a promising start.

A year later, the verdict was in: ClnFlr was a success, exceeding revenue projections by almost 50 percent.

As the team celebrated, Victor tried hard not to gloat. After all, the company was still underperforming, new leadership questioned the wisdom of innovation investment, and the quest for efficiency and optimization was crushing curiosity and creativity. Some of these battles he had fought before; some were new. But he stayed because he was still having fun fighting them.

12

Behavior
Reflect, Promote, and Repeat

I'VE NEVER been a big fan of Shakespeare, but I almost wept when I watched Kenneth Branagh deliver the St. Crispin's Day speech in the 1989 *Henry V* film during my sophomore year Intro to Shakespeare class in college:

> This story shall the good man teach his son;
> And Crispin Crispian shall ne'er go by,
> From this day to the ending of the world,
> But we in it shall be rememberèd;
> We few, we happy few, we band of brothers;
> For he to-day that sheds his blood with me
> Shall be my brother; be he ne'er so vile,
> This day shall gentle his condition;
> And gentlemen in England now a-bed
> Shall think themselves accursed they were not here,
> And hold their manhoods cheap whiles any speaks
> That fought with us upon Saint Crispin's day.

As King Henry V sat astride his horse, waving his sword defiantly and rallying his men into battle, I was transported back to moments when my teams faced equally daunting odds and the intense pride and conviction that cemented our bonds.

Innovating within a large and successful organization is nowhere near as intense or dangerous as going into battle, whether against the French in 1415 or against more modern enemies. But for us civilians, it can *feel* as if we're going into battle every time we challenge the status quo, break a rule, or dare to do something different. That's where you come in.

Like Henry V, you've grown into your role, evolving from someone who was, perhaps, seen as reckless and irresponsible into a formidable leader, now respected for your fairness and bravery. It's year 3, a critical moment in the life of your innovation team. Will you be among the 10 percent that survive or the 90 percent that are shut down?

As you, like Henry V on the eve of the Battle of Agincourt, ponder your fate, you look out on your team, reflect on all the choices that have brought you to this moment, and plan for what comes next. And again, you get out your pen and paper.

Reflect On How Far You've Come

Another year, another moment to reflect.

You know what to do: take time to quietly reflect on what you did and what you accomplished, identify learnings and changes, and make a plan.

You also know why: learning and change come from doing and reflecting on what was done and how.

Look Back

You have changed. Who you are today is not who you were when this journey began. You experienced challenges, stumbles, and successes that you never imagined. Like all innovators, you bear the scars of battles won and lost. You also have wicked, awesome stories to go with the scars.

This year, as you reflect on how you spent your time, the results you delivered, and your progress toward your aspirations, be sure to reflect on how you've changed. If that's too hard, uncomfortable, or new age, ask someone close to you how you've changed. What have you done that you never thought you'd do? What do you know now that you wish you knew at the beginning? What do you believe now that you didn't believe before? Who are you now?

The goal isn't to trigger an existential crisis. It's to recognize this experience's impact on you, the people close to you professionally and personally, and the larger communities of which you are a part. This recognition informs how you think about what's next.

Look Around

People around you are changing. They're changing because of you, the team you created, and the culture you're embedding. It's often hard to see the changes when you're in it. Just ask the frog in the boiling pot of water.

Take a moment to notice how people's behaviors changed because of your example. Do people ask questions when they are used to only taking orders? Do managers ask for input from their direct reports and engage in open conversations when communication used to flow only one way? Do senior executives who once stayed cocooned in their offices leave the building and spend time talking to customers, walking through the plant, and trying new and even competitive products?

Ask your team how they've changed since they started working on innovation. What have they learned? What are they doing that they never thought they would do? What challenges have they overcome that once seemed impossible? Do they think differently, see the world differently, or act differently?

In Victor's case, people behaved differently. Siloed, even adversarial functions worked together, collaboratively solving problems and proactively asking for input. Managers stopped micromanaging every task and decision and gave people the freedom to explore and experiment. Existing processes became simpler, and new ones emerged to reflect the ambiguity, uncertainty, and speed of early stage innovation work. Even the company's famously closed culture began to open up and acknowledge the world of ideas beyond its walls.

Of course, Victor isn't solely responsible for these changes. They were the results of dozens of people making thousands of decisions and changes each day. But he was a catalyst. As a role model, he walked the talk, questioned the status quo, encouraged creativity, and celebrated failure as learning. Could the changes have happened without him? Nope. Because if they could have, they would have.

Like Victor, you can't take full credit for these changes. They're the results of dozens of your colleagues making thousands of decisions each day. You were a catalyst. You are a role model. You showed people what change looked like and that it could be better. Could the changes have happened without you? Nope. So take credit for your role in making them happen. You earned it.

Look Forward

You're reaching the end of your three years. Victor recognized an ending when he noticed he was having less fun and felt less free than he had in his first two years leading innovation. Other people in similar roles experience the opposite when they realize that they love the relative clarity and certainty of the core business and miss the confidence they drew from it. Maybe your ending is obvious: you'll achieve your aspirations, and your innovation efforts will be wildly successful. Maybe your ending is more subtle, a nagging feeling or a soft sense of loss. However it happens, an end is near.

But how close is it? Does the work you're doing still excite you? Do you feel a sense of optimism and possibility most days? Are you working with people who inspire and motivate you? Are you learning? If the answer to any of these questions is no, the end is closer than you think.

Fear not because, as the saying goes, "Every new beginning comes from some other beginning's end."

Welcome the ending with a vision and a plan for your next beginning. After all you've learned, all you've experienced, and all you've changed, what are your new aspirations and your next great mission? What do you want to do? Who do you want to be? What impact do you want to have? And the most critical question: can you do, be, and achieve all those things where you are right now?

Like most people, Victor hoped the answer to that last question was yes, but deep down in his heart, he felt it was no. That's why the debate during the launch meeting was a relief. It allowed him to be bold and brave and experience the fun and freedom of taking a risk. If the product launch was successful, he could still do, be, and achieve what he wanted. If it wasn't, he'd have time to find his next adventure.

Stay Present

Over the past two years, you taught your team to ride the innovation bicycle. In year 1, you set the strategy and defined an initial process, then engaged your team in refining what you created, the managerial equivalent of attaching training wheels and running alongside them. In year 2, you took off the training wheels by empowering them to make some decisions and holding them accountable for results. But you still held on to the handlebars by making big decisions and protecting them from outsized reactions and repercussions. It's year 3, and the team is doing great. They're still a bit wobbly, and only a few are ready to leave the safety of the neighborhood and head out onto the city streets. You still need to be out there with them, sometimes running alongside, sometimes watching from the porch, but always within sight.

Just like a kid enjoying the new freedom of riding a bike, your team may think they don't need you, but they do. They run into new problems, just as Victor's team did when they struggled to respond to bad press from an industry group or got stuck in the legal quagmire of partnering with another company. Tools that once produced mind-blowing results and insights still work, but because more people inside and outside your company are using them, the results and insights seem less mind-blowing. Decisions that your team once made confidently become more complex and have higher stakes. Your team still needs your help, but that help is different now.

What doesn't change is their need for you to keep fighting the good fights. For years you advocated for the budget and people needed to do the work that produces the results the organization needs. How you fought those fights enhanced your reputation as someone who is tough but fair, asks for what is needed, and isn't afraid to show the consequences of what happens when it's not received. Your peers and senior executives trust and respect you. More importantly, they listen to and believe you. Your team, even your top performers, doesn't have that reputation or trust... yet. You're still the only one who can ask for what's needed, defend what you have, and get the resources and respect required to continue producing results.

Prepare the Next Generation

As for that "yet." This is when your time, energy, and attention ramp up: building the next generation of innovation leaders. For years, you led by example, mentored and coached your top performers, and created opportunities for people to try new things and gain valuable experience. Keep doing that and start sprinkling your leadership pixie dust on the next generation of innovation leaders.

Your leadership pixie dust is one part relationship, one part reputation, and one part everything unique to you. Sprinkle your pixie dust by sharing your relationships. Introduce your future leaders to your most trusted peers and advisors. Help them find and build their own circle of trusted counselors. It's also critical to help them go beyond the people in their immediate teams, business units, and even countries to build new connections. Connecting and building relationships comes naturally to some people but not to others. In fact, your hardest workers probably struggle the most because they believe that good work and great results matter more than anything else. By now, you know that part of leadership is teaching, and that means that it falls to you to help your people understand that hard work is absolutely necessary but sadly not sufficient to achieve their goals and aspirations. Success requires good work, great results, and solid relationships.

As for your reputation pixie dust, if you're going to keep moving up, it's gotta fall on some of your top people so they can eventually fill your shoes. Bring them to meetings with you. First, the presentations that are unlikely to be controversial where they can meaningfully contribute. Then the tougher ones where debates occur so they can listen, observe, and maybe chime in with a fact or two. Ultimately, bring them into the brutal, knock-down-drag-out battles that you've sheltered them from for years.

You may be tempted to keep protecting them, to ask them to leave the room when things get heated, but don't. Victor didn't ask the team to leave when the debate was raging and when he threw down his offer. He knew that everything happening involved and affected them, and he hoped that one day, one of the people watching the scene unfold would be in his role. He knew that it was only fair to show them the highs and lows of the job so they knew what they were up against and could decide if they wanted to take it on.

Repeat. Repeat. Repeat.

"For a year and a half, I've been saying we are one team," the executive director of an operating unit lamented during a Zoom call. "In every monthly all-staff meeting. In every all-staff email. In every leadership team meeting. We are one team. One team. Then today, at the end of our nineteenth all-staff meeting, someone approached me and said, 'Thanks for saying we're one team. I hadn't heard that before, and I think it's important.'"

I wanted to reach through the screen and hug him, but all I could do was smile, nod, and try to comfort him with assurances that a year and a half is pretty quick. Most change messages take years to sink in.

It's hard not to take moments like the one my client described personally. When you say something over and over so many times that you're sick of saying it, it's natural to imagine that everyone else is sick of hearing it. And if they're not sick of hearing it, it's because they're not listening. And if they're not listening, it's because they don't care, don't respect you, or have no intention of changing to act in a way consistent with the values and culture you're establishing (or some combination of all three).

But it's not personal. It's not because they don't care. It's not because they're not listening. It's because you are one person delivering one message in a day filled with people delivering messages, tasks demanding actions, and problems requiring solutions. They heard you, and then something else that was more relevant, important, and urgent popped up.

You spend all day with your messages about innovation. They spend one minute. You spend time reading, learning, and talking about innovation best practices. They spend time reading, learning, and talking about best practices in their jobs (which have little if anything to do with yours).

Instead of succumbing to the frustration of screaming into the void, look at it another way. What are the biggest challenges in the supply chain right now? What are the latest marketing best practices? What new regulations are about to take effect that could materially affect financial reporting practices? It's okay if you don't know the answers, but I can guarantee that your supply chain, marketing, and finance colleagues know the answers. They spend time reading, learning, and talking about these topics because it's their job to know the answers, and they're really frustrated that you're not listening.

So, take a deep breath, and keep talking about innovation. Keep communicating what innovation is and why it's essential to the organization and everyone in it. Keep reminding people that innovation isn't an event, a hobby, or a silver bullet. Keep educating people about why the tools used to manage the core business are entirely and dangerously wrong for driving innovation.

There's no such thing as too early or too often regarding innovation education and communication. So, keep at it. Your audience will hear you when the message becomes relevant to them and their work. They may even remember it.

There's no such thing as too early or too often

regarding innovation education and communication.

TL;DR Year 3 Behavior

There is no such thing as too early or too often in innovation.

Reflect on how far you've come. Take a moment to acknowledge all that you've accomplished:

- Look back and recognize how your experience affected you professionally and personally.
- Look around at how your work affected your team and the organization.
- Look forward to what you want to achieve next.

Stay present. Your team needs you, even if they don't think they do.

- Prepare your team for the new challenges they will face.
- Continue to defend your team and fight for resources because the organization continues to struggle to balance innovation and operations.
- Nurture the next generation of innovation leaders by making introductions, teaching them to build connections, and sprinkling your reputational pixie dust on your top performers.

Constantly communicate because the moment you get sick of saying something is the first time it's heard.

- Communicate what innovation is and why it's essential to the organization.
- Remind people that innovation isn't an event, a hobby, or a silver bullet.
- Educate people about why the tools used to manage the core business are entirely and dangerously wrong for driving innovation.

13

Architecture
Challenges, Strategies, and Cynics

AFTER TWO YEARS of building, adjusting, adapting, and rein-
forcing, your innovation architecture is rock solid, operating like a
well-oiled machine and producing results.

Your team is collaborative and creative, demonstrates an entrepreneurial spirit and an ownership mindset, and isn't afraid to fail
because they're more excited to learn. Most importantly, they're
producing results. Real, meaningful, revenue-generating results.

Your process guides the team, focuses their energies, and keeps
them moving forward efficiently and quickly. You established governance that makes it clear who makes decisions, when, and what
the decisions are based on.

You continue to educate and communicate like a fiend. From
scheduled updates and impromptu hallway conversations with
executives and stakeholders to presentations and email blasts to
the broader organization, you explain what innovation is, why it's
important, how it's done, and what it produces. There were moments
when you thought you couldn't bear to say any of these things even

one more time. Those were also the moments when someone sat up, gasped, and said, "I didn't know that. Now I get it!"

Your work here is done. It's time to hand the blueprints over to the next generation of leaders and let them make the updates and improvements that are, no doubt, required. You can finally ease up just a bit. Right?

Sorry, no. You and your team are about to face new enemies and challenges. If it's any comfort, you face these enemies and challenges because, as French writer and politician Victor Hugo wrote, "it is the story of every man who has done a great deed or created a new idea. It is the cloud which thunders around everything which shines. Fame must have enemies, as light must have gnats."

The Belt-Tightening

You're halfway through the year when the request comes in for everyone to pitch in a bit of their budget to shore up the struggling product line or business unit. Senior executives encourage everyone to be "good corporate citizens" and return some of their budget to the corporate coffers. No matter how the request is positioned, the result is the same—you have less money.

It happens every year, so you knew the request was coming, and you played the game. You padded your budget request and front-loaded your spending. Or maybe you played it straight, asked for just what you needed, and reminded people every chance you got that your request was conservative and that your team was starting the year with not a penny to spare.

Your approach doesn't matter. The request still comes.

Be prepared. Like Victor, identify what can be cut without significantly impacting your ability to deliver promised results. Understand where there is flexibility and what activities can quickly turn on and off. Resist the urge to make many little cuts across your entire portfolio that serve only to diminish the change and impact of the project, and brace yourself to make significant cuts, like killing a project.

When someone asks you to be a good corporate citizen, negotiate. Refusing to cut your budget to shore up someone else's is politically dangerous and results in you losing your budget and the relationships and goodwill you spent years cultivating. However, you don't need to take the first offer and give everything they requested. They don't know your budget the way you do and don't understand the implications of the cuts they are asking for. You have the opportunity and responsibility to help them understand those things and find a number you can both live with. I've never seen someone rewarded for cutting their budget. I have seen people punished (not promoted, lower bonuses) for not delivering results because they cut their funding.

The Strategic Shift

This challenge occurs less frequently but is more powerful than belt-tightening and comes in many forms.

One form manifests itself as the arrival of a new senior executive. As days turn into weeks, they are compelled to make their mark on the company, make it evident that a new era is beginning, and that they are the perfect leader for this moment. It's not long before they unveil a new strategy.

The other form occurs when the economy slows or the market becomes uncertain. Executives run to strategies that promise safety and frugality. Expansion halts as resources are gathered into core markets, and innovation investments are judged as ill timed and too risky. Success requires doing more with less, not building what's next.

No matter the cause of the shift, the new strategy challenges the merits and importance of innovation. Executives point to declining revenues or shifting market dynamics and assert that now is not the right time to innovate. Some believe that continued investment is irresponsible. They claim that the organization's foundation is crumbling and that anything that doesn't mend it is wasteful. They reassure you that the time for innovation is coming, but first, as stewards of the business, it's more important to be safe and to fix the organization's foundation, its core business.

As the innovation leader, you get to explain that safety is an illusion and innovation *is* the fix.

The organization's foundation is crumbling because the ground beneath it is shifting. Technology is evolving more quickly, and in more directions, than executives imagined. Consumer preferences and behaviors are changing faster than ever before. Economic cycles are speeding up, financial markets are creating new patterns, and global events like wars and pandemics are becoming all too frequent.

The way to fix the foundation isn't by mending the organization with the same tools and materials used to build it. It's to adapt the foundation to the new ground upon which it sits. That's the purpose of innovation. Innovation isn't *a* fix. It is *the* fix.

People expect this argument from you. After all, you're not exactly an unbiased participant. They don't expect that you have results that prove you're right. The work you did over the past two years and the results you started generating last year are evidence that innovation is a fix that is already working in the organization. Innovation investments are no longer speculative; they're delivering tangible results, and revenue is on the horizon if not already coming in. Innovation is no longer the island of misfit toys; it's a high-performing team that is the envy of competitors. Innovation culture is no longer a recruiting message or a "mandatory fun" event. It's the way the organization operates.

Tell this story and then show that it is true. Show the data and the charts. Play the testimonials from consumers and channel partners.

Pass around the prototypes. Share the quotes from frustrated and jealous competitors and the case studies of executives who had the wisdom to invest in innovation when no one else was and, as a result, stabilized the business and propelled it to rapid growth and sustained market leadership.

The Cynic

Cynics are everywhere. They were quiet in year 1 because innovation was a priority. Their doubts became whispers in year 2 as results were slow to come in. If you don't have revenue in year 3, those whispers increase in volume and become shouts if there's nothing on the horizon by the end of the year. And you're in the 90 percent that don't make it to year 4.

Cynics aren't born; they're created. Usually, long before you took on this role, personal experiences and workplace cultures left these individuals feeling mistreated. As most people do in professional settings, they pushed these feelings down way deep inside, gritted their teeth, and got on with things. But the feelings never went away. They festered and mutated into feelings of paranoia and perceptions of injustice in every decision and statement. Eventually, these thoughts and perceptions spilled into their interactions with others as they engaged in "preemptive strikes" like dishonest negotiations, cheating, and cruelty. Ironically, they were rewarded for these behaviors, benefiting from the "cynical-genius illusion" in which their peers "view their cynicism as hard-earned wisdom and consider anyone who doesn't share it to be naive."

This last part is why cynics are so powerful: others see them as intelligent and savvy role models. And it's not just a few others. In research out of Tilburg University, 70 percent of participants perceived cynics as generally smarter than non-cynics, a perception not backed up by intelligence tests. Given this majority perception, it's no wonder that cynicism is considered an emotional contagion capable of rapidly spreading negativity, distrust, disengagement, and even cruelty throughout an organization.

You won't win them over with strategy, data, or results because cynicism isn't logical. It's emotional. You must win the cynic's heart before your results can win their head. Doing both is one of your greatest challenges as an innovation leader. Happily, the key to winning is one of innovation's most foundational and powerful tools and an instinct you spent the last two years developing, role modeling, and teaching—empathy.

Talk to them and understand their point of view based on their experiences. Don't try convincing them they're mistaken or not seeing the whole picture. Listen and empathize with them, not because you think they're right but because you, too, have experienced frustration and unfairness in your life. When they feel heard, share your goals for innovation and discuss your commitment to ensuring that everyone feels valued and respected. Through stories, illustrate how you and your team believe you're achieving these goals, and then ask for their ideas on how to improve.

Will this conversation end in hugs and an exchange of friendship bracelets? Probably not, though stranger things have happened.

Will you have to have this conversation again? Most likely.

But nothing changes or improves until you have it the first time.

Continue to walk the talk. Remember that the cynic is created when someone promises one thing and does another. Demonstrate the behaviors and emotions you want people to follow: ask questions, admit when you don't know something, take a deep breath before you react, assume best intentions, and stay optimistic. Eliminate the feelings of distrust and secrecy that allow cynicism to spread by quickly and transparently sharing news and decisions and the why behind them. Keep producing and sharing results, always explaining why the cynics are better off because of innovation's work.

Demonstrate the behaviors you want people to follow: ask questions, admit when you don't know something, and take a deep breath before you react.

TL;DR Year 3 Architecture

Innovation is all fun and games until someone loses a resource. Be prepared, be flexible, be unafraid to step on toes.

Prepare for budget cuts so you can defend against them.

- Request a budget that is on the high side of reasonable.
- Work with your team to identify where and how you can cut if (when) necessary.
- Negotiate cuts knowing the request is based on people's understanding of the core business, not innovation.

Be flexible when the operational environment changes because it's the only way to survive and succeed.

- Look out for economic downturns, geopolitical uncertainty, and the arrival of new senior executives.
- Demonstrate innovation's strategic and financial importance to reduce the risk that others deem it too uncertain and funnel its resources to safer operational activities.
- Help your peers and executives confront and lead through the tension of balancing operations *and* innovation.

Reinforce that innovation is happening.

- Reach out to people who feel mistreated so they don't become cynical and see unfairness and injustice everywhere.
- Call out cynicism when you see it to save people and the culture from falling prey to the "cynical-genius illusion."
- Work to win people's hearts and heads by offering empathy, connection, and patience in addition to data and logic.

Culture
Movements, Events, and Partners

IT'S A HOT summer day in the foothills. The grass near the stage is lush and green, and on the other side of the chain-link fence, the crystal-clear lake glistens cool and calm. Hundreds of people have gathered for an outdoor music festival, and the crowd is relaxed, nodding along to the music emanating from the speakers.

Then he shows up. Some lone nut in navy blue shorts and no shirt, wriggling and flailing about in a manner that can only loosely be described as dancing.

People slowly back away, dragging their chairs and picnic blankets with them. Eventually, the dancer is alone, with nothing but twenty feet of grass around him in every direction. He is unfazed. He continues to revolve and wave his arms wildly over his head.

Suddenly, another person runs up to him, stopping a mere ten feet away. He, too, begins to wriggle and flail. Within seconds, the lone nut spots his follower and rushes over. They clasp hands and dance together. Eventually, the first follower calls out to his friends, waving them over and reassuring them that it is safe.

A third person joins, and the dance expands to include somersaults, high kicks, and other forms of rudimentary gymnastics. Within seconds, they are joined by a fourth, fifth, and sixth person. The twenty-foot circle of empty grass that once surrounded the lone nut is now filled with people dancing wildly and with fierce abandon.

What began as a lone nut became a movement.

Two years ago, you were a lone nut. Then your team became your first followers, and you greeted them as equals because the culture you wanted to create wasn't about you. It was about innovation. Last year, you and your team invited others into your organization and showed them how to follow. This year is the tipping point. This year, you turn your momentum into a movement.

Create a Crowd

The story you just read is based on Derek Sivers's fantastic TED Talk, "How to Start a Movement," a two-minute and fifty-two-second burst of insight, laughs, and brilliant advice. He says:

> A movement must be public. It's important to show not just the leader but the followers, because you find that new followers emulate the followers, not the leader...
>
> Notice that as more people join in, it's less risky. So those that were sitting on the fence before now have no reason not to. They won't stand out, they won't be ridiculed, but they will be part of the in-crowd if they hurry. Over the next minute, you'll see all of those that prefer to stick with the crowd [rush in] because eventually they would be ridiculed for not joining in. And that's how you make a movement.

To make a movement, you need to get people off the fence, and in large organizations, the best way to do that is through HR programs. I'm sure many people rolled their eyes when they read that last sentence, but hear me out. Nothing says "This is official and safe" better than an HR-approved training program or other development opportunity. When companies offer classes and workshops on innovation tools or establish an "innovation university" to help employees deepen their skills and build expertise, you know that innovation has arrived.

Other organizations go even further. For example, as Hope's team and responsibilities grew, she started an exchange program in which a handful of carefully selected people from the core business joined her innovation team for six months to one year, allowing them to gain hands-on experience working rapidly in a highly ambiguous and uncertain environment. I know of at least two companies that offer secondments, essentially programs that allow top performers to spend up to a year working at a startup or in another company's innovation team with the expectation that they return and teach their colleagues what they've learned.

As you continue to teach and support innovators throughout the organization, teach them how to teach others. After all, in many ways, they're like kids who just learned something exciting and new, and they want to tell people all about it. Remember "new followers emulate the followers, not the leader."

Events, Not Theaters

Innovation is not an event. However, an event can lead to innovation if done correctly.

Unfortunately, it rarely is.

That is how innovation theater happens.

"Innovation theater" is a term coined by Steve Blank to describe any act undertaken with the promise of innovation that doesn't deliver business impact.

If a knot appeared in your stomach as you read that, you're not alone. Innovation events—like shark tanks and hackathons, field

Innovation is not an event. However, an event can lead to innovation if done correctly.

trips to "innovation hot zones" to meet with startups and other innovators, and boot camps to develop new offerings with minimal investment—start with the best intentions but often devolve into innovation theater.

It doesn't have to be that way.

Step 1: Start at the End

Like every project and initiative the company invests in, start with the end in mind and define what success looks like. More specifically, since innovation is something new that creates value, determine the value the event must create and by when. And make sure everyone agrees.

To illustrate this, let's check in with Faith as her team starts its year 3 work. As part of Faith's focus on creating and launching new business models, she asked one of her direct reports, Pru, to design a three-day hackathon. Having studied successful hackathons, especially Google's design sprint approach, Pru quickly devised a plan and scheduled the event.

Luckily, she slowed down just enough to ask what success looked like. In Pru's mind, success meant that everyone in the organization participated. However, Faith viewed success as radically new thinking that produced at least one project capable of launching in three years and generating $100 million in new revenue.

That definition changed everything.

Pru needed a new plan.

Step 2: The End Determines the Means

When you understand the business impact you need to deliver, you can work backward to define the path, remembering that the event is only a tiny part of the journey. However, to design the path, you must first identify your assumptions.

With her original plan blown to smithereens, Pru started over by asking herself, "What must be true to deliver Faith's definition of success?" To successfully get radically new ideas, she realized it must be true that they:

- Ask for them
- Define what is and isn't a radically new idea that can be a source of growth in three to five years
- Provide information, perspectives, and tools to help people think out that far

For the hackathon to successfully result in a project that drives growth in three to five years, Pru determined it must be true that they:

- Work on top ideas after the hackathon
- Dedicate resources to explore winning ideas
- Have a long-term strategy, so they know roughly where they want to be as a company in three to five years
- Have a member of leadership involved to guide the teams

Like most people planning an innovation event, the first part—giving teams a focus for their creativity—was relatively easy. The second part—maintaining momentum by ensuring that money and people were available immediately after the hackathon to continue the work—was not.

Step 3: Make the Means Happen—Especially the Hard Ones

This step is the difference between innovation theater and innovation success.

Most planners are overwhelmed by the organizational challenges involved in maintaining momentum after the event, especially given the uncertainty of what emerges and who needs to be involved. Instead of facing the challenge head-on, they ask their peers to promise to support winning projects by allocating a few people to the team if necessary.

Promises aren't plans.

When you rely on promises, you build a theater.

When you make plans, you design for success.

Pru planned. She wrote a list of everything that needed to be true to maintain momentum and ensure that work continued immediately after the hackathon and was supported for at least six months. Among the dozens of items on this list were three that made her very, very nervous:

1 Move the winning team(s) out of their current roles within thirty days so they can work on their project full-time.

2 Dedicate budget for six months of development and testing.

3 Move the winning team back into current or new roles if the idea doesn't work.

These three items were mission critical to achieving Faith's definition of success, but Pru didn't think they were possible. At their next meeting, Pru gave Faith a choice: redefine success to something that didn't require post-event organizational or financial commitment, or use her positional power to guarantee that people and budget would be dedicated to a new and undefined project within thirty days of the event's end.

Faith chose the latter and worked with HR and the managers of the hackathon participants to develop realistic plans to extricate current team members and either reallocate their work to other team members or backfill them with new employees. Pulling these plans together wasn't easy, and there were times Pru thought she was about to be proven correct as people declared that what they were asking for was impossible. But Faith persevered, even delaying (but refusing to cancel) the hackathon for three months to get all the requirements and guarantees in place.

While Faith worked on the post-hackathon plan, Pru focused on what needed to happen before and during the event. She created an internal marketing campaign to drive awareness of the event, its purpose, and the prize. She carefully composed the messaging, so people understood they were signing up for more than an event. If they won, they were signing up for six months to a year of developing their idea. All of this was in stark contrast to the "Do whatever you want and go back to your old job on Monday" hackathons of the past. As a result, some people chose not to participate, but those who did worked with more focus, energy, and commitment than ever before.

Step 4: Let Go

With so much invested in getting to the event, let alone all the plans and investment to enable what happens after, it's tempting to script the work, believing that giving people a process to follow, tools and templates to use, and milestones to hit will increase the odds of success.

They don't.

They increase the odds of failure.

A 2021 study by professors at Harvard, the University of Virginia, and Tel Aviv University found that the most successful hackathon teams spent little time or energy planning and coordinating their work.

In 2015 and 2016, two US-based makerspaces hosted seventy-two-hour hackathons to develop and deliver a functioning assistive technology product prototype. Participants didn't know each other before the event and had no relevant experience or expertise in assistive technology. Each person chose from thirteen projects on which to work, ranging from helping blind people operate devices to assisting people without limbs perform daily tasks.

At the end of the hackathon, three of the thirteen teams presented durable prototypes that used both electrical and mechanical elements to function. Three teams presented less advanced and less durable but still functional prototypes. Seven teams produced nothing.

This is the opposite of what you would expect based on how the teams started.

The seven teams that failed to produce even a nonfunctioning prototype started by condensing the innovation process into a seventy-two-hour time frame and created a plan "to bring order and coherence to the chaotic process and establish a shared approach, avoiding wasted time due to lack of alignment." In the first hour, they defined their prototype based on their understanding of the problem, broke it down into its element parts, and agreed on expectations for each. They prioritized the work and assigned clear roles and responsibilities to team members. When problems arose, the team reconvened to problem-solve and collectively determine a new course of action.

In contrast, the six teams that produced functioning prototypes allowed their process to emerge. Simply starting to work, the team learned, adapted, and collaborated flexibly and open-mindedly. The approach was emergent, but it wasn't chaotic. The three teams that produced the most advanced prototypes demonstrated what the researchers termed "adaptive coordination" that "involved swift sensing and adjusting, quick iterations for providing sporadic updates, and creating quick feedback loops that gradually increased alignment over time." This approach stands in stark contrast to the full coordination of the seven failed teams and the minimal coordination of the teams with basic functional prototypes.

Pru did exactly what all corporate innovators (and their consultants) are trained to do. She set a clear schedule with timed milestones, interrupted creative work to brief teams on a new tool that would be helpful for the next phase of work, and armed them with templates, best practices, and example deliverables to boost their odds of success when presenting to the senior leadership "shark tank." Her results mirrored those of the researchers. A few teams developed early but uninspiring prototypes, but the majority developed beautiful slides describing inspiring ideas well beyond current technology.

Executives were wowed by the ideas and disappointed in the prototypes. Pru sensed they were about to reward the most inspiring but least practical idea with three months of funding, but she knew she couldn't directly call out the CEO's flawed logic. She rushed to find Faith.

Within seconds, Faith entered the room to "check in" on how deliberations were proceeding. Before the CEO could tell her they picked a winner, she gently reminded them that they had agreed that a successful hackathon would produce at least one project capable of launching in three years and generating $100 million in new revenue. "Do we have at least one project that fits that bill?" she innocently inquired despite knowing full well that they did, but it wasn't the winner they had selected.

The CEO nodded solemnly, slowly realizing that he and the rest of the shark tank had gotten caught up in the excitement and energy of new ideas. Afraid to show that he had forgotten the purpose of the event and its importance to the company, he said that the judges were narrowing in on a winner, but he'd like Faith's input before making a final decision. Smiling, she steered them toward a team with a functioning but uninspiring prototype that, if successful, had the power to transform the business.

With the right decision made, Faith excused herself from the room, winking at Pru as she left.

Step 5: Deliver

A lot can happen between the day you first conceive of an event and the day that the event ends. But nothing short of going out of business changes your plan for what happens after the event.

Your post-event plan is a promise to the organization to continue to invest in innovation and stands as tangible evidence of your commitment. If you cancel that plan and break your promise, you lose all credibility and destroy all progress toward embedding a culture of innovation in your organization.

As extreme as that sounds, it's true. Actions speak louder than words.

Despite the CEO's momentary wobble on what *should* win the hackathon, he didn't wobble at all on the commitments he made for dedicated staffing and funding for the team to continue developing their idea. Though the team fell short of its three-month goals, it had made sufficient progress to convince management that the project was technically feasible within three to five years and financially viable, thus earning another three months of funding and support.

Partners

With all your work managing an innovation team and building a culture of innovation, it's hard to find the time or energy to look outside the organization. This is especially true if your organization is already considered a leader in its industry. Yes, it's challenging, but in the words of Ferris Bueller, "Life moves pretty fast. If you don't stop and look around once in a while, you could miss it."

Adopting an open-innovation practice enables you to discover new technologies, approaches, and solutions to accelerate your progress. According to *The Innovator's DNA*, the main quality shared by all great innovators is their ability to connect two disparate pieces of innovation into something new, a process exemplified by Steve Jobs's application of his calligraphy class to computer fonts. Encouraging people to look outside and rewarding them for making nonobvious connections is the first step in building the innovation behaviors that become an innovation culture.

Going further, structures like P&G's famous Connect + Develop and multiple companies' corporate venture capital create formal pathways through which new technologies, offerings, and even business models enter the organization and become part of the balance sheet.

The main quality shared by all great innovators is their ability to connect **two disparate pieces of innovation into something new.**

TL;DR Year 3 Culture

You're no longer a lone nut. You're leading a movement.

Expand beyond culture creation to build and spread a movement.

- Encourage your first followers (your team) and your second followers (year 2 innovators) to engage and teach the next wave of followers.

- Make innovation safe by partnering with HR to teach innovation tools and mindsets and provide opportunities to work as an innovator.

Design and deliver events that drive the movement forward, instead of being theater.

- Design events by working backward from the end and asking, "What must be true?" to ensure that the events generate the desired results.

- Keep doing the opposite of your instincts and allow people to create and define their own approach to innovation during events. (Research shows it works.)

- When you commit to supporting people, teams, and ideas after an event, deliver. If you don't, you lose trust and goodwill and create cynics.

Ferris Bueller was right: "Life moves pretty fast. If you don't stop and look around once in a while, you could miss it."

- Establish structures for open innovation to facilitate bringing outside ideas into your organization and onto the balance sheet.

- Reward people for discovering new things and creating new ideas by connecting ideas from different fields.

Know Your Innovation Events

LIKE SO MANY TERMS, "innovation theater" started as a memorable way to call attention to activities that look innovation-y on the surface but that don't have the resources or commitment required to deliver something new that creates value (i.e., innovation). Over time, however, the term has become weaponized. Now it's not unusual to hear skeptical executives label every innovation event as "theater" even if it's been thoughtfully designed to produce strategically sound actionable ideas likely to generate measurable value.

Here are the most common types of innovation events.

- **Brainstorm:** A spontaneous session in which a group of people generate as many ideas as possible on a specific topic or challenge

- **Idea contest:** An event or ongoing program in which employees are asked to submit their ideas, typically to a central team for evaluation

- **Hackathon:** A time-limited event (typically twenty-four to forty-eight hours) during which teams collaborate intensely to create a prototype solution to a challenge

- **Shark tank:** A pitch event in which individuals or teams present their ideas, prototypes, or business plans to a small panel of judges for potential funding or implementation

- **Field trip:** An organized trip to an external location like a startup, customer site, or consumer home for the purposes of being inspired, gaining perspective, and generating new ideas

- **Incubator:** A program or structure focused on guiding ideas through the front end of the innovation process (problem discovery and diagnosis, idea generation, concept refinement, and initial business plan validation)

- **Accelerator:** A program or structure focused on guiding validated early stage projects through the latter part of the innovation process (discovery-driven planning, experimentation, and pilot markets)

All of these events have the potential to be innovation theater. They also have the potential to be the origin of a breakthrough innovation that creates tremendous value, accelerates your organization's growth, or alters the future of your industry. While there's no way to guarantee that the event is the latter, there are signs.

To minimize the chances of being innovation theater, an event must offer *all* of the following:

- Specific strategies, problems, or topics for which ideas are wanted and an explanation as to why it is an organizational priority

- Guardrails that define what makes an idea attractive (e.g., market opportunity, time to launch, resources required, and estimated value created)

- Clear and concise evaluation criteria and transparent evaluation process

- Timeline and process for responding to *all* submissions

- Clear and concrete next steps for top ideas

One More Thing...

WE STARTED with the facts: 99.9 percent of incubated ideas never reach the market, 95 percent of innovations fail in the market, and 90 percent of innovation teams are shut down in the first three years.

Then you learned the ABCs of Innovation—what they are, why they're essential, and how to apply them with your stakeholders and team to achieve your goals.

You read stories of real-life innovation leaders like you who applied the ABCs and defied the odds, joining the ranks of the few who survived beyond year 3, launched new offerings, and succeeded in the market for years after launch.

Before you run off, there's one more thing to learn from one more person's story.

July 22, 2005

My mom was as close to a pied piper as you could ever meet. She loved kids and dedicated her life to teaching preschool. Kids loved her back. When we ran errands or walked through Cleveland to get to an Indians game, it wasn't unusual to see a child let go of their parent's hand, walk over, and take my mom's, even though she was a complete stranger. When that happened, she just walked them back to their parents, knelt down, took their hand from hers, and placed it back in their parent's hand. When she stood up, she would smile down at the kid, the kid would smile back, and you would swear that their shared look reflected a close bond.

My sister inherited some of my mom's magic. I did not. I'm more like my dad in that I tend to approach small children as if they are sticky, incomprehensible aliens destined to make a mess of my clothes and my day. Which is why I still don't know what possessed me to do what I did on July 22, 2005.

My mom passed away suddenly on July 18, and my dad, sister, and I were greeting people as they arrived for her wake. In addition to her friends and colleagues, a surprising number of kids came to pay their respects. Kids she taught in preschool, kids who planned to be in her class that coming year, even teenagers who'd had her as a Sunday School teacher years earlier. But there was one kid, a little girl with jet-black hair, whom I will never forget.

She was a wreck. She was a bigger mess of tears, snot, and sobs than any other person I saw that week, which is saying something. And she seemed to be alone. After a few minutes of glancing over at her as I greeted people, I stepped out of line and walked over to her. Kneeling down to make eye contact, I gently placed my hand on her shoulder and asked if she was okay.

"Your mom changed my life."

I admit that it took all my strength not to roll my eyes. This girl was six, maybe seven. There's not a whole lot of life to change. The entire situation was getting more dramatic than I had the patience for, even on my best days. But this kid was a mess, and my mom loved kids, so to honor my mom, I asked her what she meant.

She explained that when she was four years old and in my mom's class, she had difficulty making friends. It was enough of an issue that her parents considered pulling her out of school and homeschooling her or sending her away to a "special school." But she loved to sing and my mom sang with her.

Let me be very clear about something: my mom could not sing. Like the rest of our family, this woman could not carry a tune in a bucket. So, I almost burst out laughing at the idea of my mom spending all day singing with this girl.

Somehow, I stifled my laughter and kept nodding. The girl explained that because someone sang with her, she grew confident enough to start talking to people. She made friends. Her parents didn't pull her out of school. They enrolled her in kindergarten. Now, she loved school, had friends, and was in the school choir. All because my mom sang with her.

When she finished her story, I thanked her, hugged her, and told her my mom would be proud of her. As I stood and walked back to the receiving line, I realized that my mom was the most successful person I knew because she had changed one person's life. After all that I had done, seen, and learned, it wasn't until that moment that I understood what success is: changing one person's life, even if it means embarrassing yourself.

You Define Success

Throughout this book, I've written about what it takes to succeed, to be among the 10 percent of corporate innovators who survive the first three years, build sustainable innovation capabilities and cultures, and launch innovations that succeed in the market.

As year 3 comes to a close, you learn your fate. Maybe you're leading a team in the 10 percent that survive to continue innovating in year 4. Perhaps you're off to bigger and better things. Maybe you're in the majority of innovation leaders who get to start again.

To be honest, it doesn't matter.

It doesn't matter because whatever happens, you're a success.

You taught someone courage when you demonstrated the importance of always doing your best, working your hardest, and never giving up on your dream, even though there was no guarantee that you would survive the first three years. You inspired someone to take a risk every time you broke the rules, challenged authority, worked hard, and did the right thing. You succeeded because you changed someone's life by showing them that they are capable of far more than they ever dreamed.

Over the past three years, you proved that when people believe in themselves and their potential, anything is possible—even innovating within a large and successful organization.

Congratulations! You're an innovation leader.

You deserve a cookie. (May I recommend chocolate chip?)

You succeeded because you changed someone's life by showing them that **they are capable of far more than they ever dreamed.**

Acknowledgments

FOR AS LONG AS I can remember, I've dreamed of being an author. As a kid, I loved to write and illustrate stories, but as I grew older, the romantic notion of sitting alone in a rickety, cozy cottage, tapping out a novel while the angry waves of the sea crashed against the cliffs below became ever more appealing to my introverted self.

Then I actually wrote a book.

It's not a novel (though I did take some liberties with the stories of Hope, Faith, and Victor). I didn't write it in a cottage near the sea (though parts were written on the balcony of a condo overlooking the Gulf of Mexico). And I sure as heck didn't write it alone.

First, I must thank my family. Mom, Dad, and Diana were the first people to believe that I could and would write a book. They encouraged and supported my writing throughout my life, from Young Authors to Power of the Pen. They were the ultimate cheerleaders, and while this book won't achieve my dream of displacing *Moby Dick* from the canon of English literature, thus sparing generations of teenagers from having to read that stupid book, maybe the next one will.

Thank you to my husband, Matt. He picked up daily cheerleading duties and took them to the next level. Every groan of "I'm going to write" was met with an enthusiastic "Good for you!" He honored my request to never ask how the book was coming along or where I was in the process, but he always stopped whatever he was doing to listen when I was ready to talk. I cannot imagine a more supportive partner in writing or in life, and for that, I am eternally grateful.

Thank you to my writing support group. My accountability bae 4 life, Kate Dixon, started every week by listening to me whine about the writing process and offering her patient wisdom as the author of two books. Thank you to Curtis Chan, award-winning assistant professor of management and organization at Boston College, for providing invaluable advice on the book as a whole, sharing sources to back up or correct my hypotheses, and forgiving me for tormenting him when he was on my project team as an analyst fresh out of Harvard College.

Thank you to my beta readers Brittany, Grace, Heather, and Stacie, who read the second draft of this book (no one will ever see the horrendous first draft) and offered their kind, thoughtful, and supremely helpful feedback. This book is better because of you. Thanks to my alumnae circle (especially Amy, Lyn, Barbara, and Linda) and Forum v (I'd list you, but the first rule of Forum v is we don't talk about Forum v), who also listened to my whining and responded with unwavering encouragement.

Thank you to my coaches. To Dianne Argyris, who was the first person to encourage me to start my own business, and to Marshall Goldsmith who was even more emphatic in his encouragement for the few hours we were seatmates on a flight to Boston—and who has continued his generosity and support by writing the foreword. To Rochelle Seltzer and Christine Kane, who helped me rediscover my voice and build MileZero, and to David A. Fields, who kicked off this adventure in February 2023 when he uttered the words, "Have you ever thought about writing a book?" From that moment to this one, he has been a steadfast guide, and I am deeply grateful for his honesty and advice.

Thank you to Hope, Faith, and Victor for trusting me and collaborating with me to show the world that it is possible to innovate within large and successful organizations. Thank you to all my clients and my collaborators. Many of the lessons we learned together are sprinkled throughout this book, whereas our misadventures—while also informative and definitely amusing—are not. Thanks to my Swiffer colleagues, especially my R&D counterpart and fellow yak-hair co-conspirator Matt Nitowski, for making my first years in the "real world" both fun and the foundation for everything that came next.

And finally, thank *you*, dear reader, for all that you do. For believing in the power of ideas and knowing that they're only as good as the action you take and the value they create. For seeing the creative potential in everyone, whether they're big thinkers or skilled refiners, and creating the space for them to show and share their brilliance. For knowing that better *is* possible, being brave enough to make it happen, and being bold enough to know that no is the start of the conversation, not the end.

Cookies for everyone!

(Yes, they'll be chocolate chip.)

Notes

1. What's the Problem?

p. 4   *0.1 percent of ideas developed by companies launch:* Harsh Vardhan, "Why So Many Product Ideas Fail?" Medium, September 26, 2020, medium.com/product-center-of-excellence/why-so-many-product -ideas-fail-6a90af06c15a.

p. 4   *Less than 50 percent of these launched ideas achieve $1 million in sales:* Laura Furstenthal et al., "Committed Innovators: How Masters of Essentials Outperform," McKinsey & Company, June 9, 2022, mckinsey.com/capabilities/strategy-and-corporate-finance/our-insights/ committed-innovators-how-masters-of-essentials-outperform.

p. 6   *researched corporate innovators' careers:* Scott Kirsner, "How Long Do Corporate Innovation Jobs Last, and What Happens Next?" InnoLead, January 23, 2019, innovationleader.com/topics/articles-and-content -by-topic/innovation-metrics/how-long-do-corporate-innovation-jobs -last-and-what-happens-next.

p. 6   *90 percent of corporate innovation labs and incubators fail within three years:* Brian Solis et al., "The Innovation Game: Why and How Businesses Are Investing in Innovation Centers," Capgemini Consulting/Altimeter, 2015, slideshare.net/slideshow/the-innovation-game-why-and-how- businesses-are-investing-in-innovation-centers/64787305.

Know Your Innovation Leadership Toolkit

p. 21   *suggests handwriting is a better tool than typing:* Aya S. Ihara et al., "Advantage of Handwriting over Typing on Learning Words: Evidence from an N400 Event-Related Potential Index," *Frontiers in Human*

Neuroscience 15 (June 2021): 679191, doi.org/10.3389/fnhum.2021 .679191; Maggy McGloin, "What You Miss When You Take Notes on Your Laptop," *Harvard Business Review*, July 31, 2015, hbr.org/2015/07/ what-you-miss-when-you-take-notes-on-your-laptop.

p. 21   *Demands more cognitive engagement that typing:* Jo Banks, "8 Reasons Why Handwriting Is Better Than Typing…" LinkedIn, June 9, 2023, linkedin .com/pulse/8-reasons-why-handwriting-better-than-typing-jo-banks.

p. 22   *Encourages critical thinking and allows for better memory retention:* "The Benefits of Handwriting vs. Typing," Pens.com, April 2016, pens.com/ blog/the-benefits-of-handwriting-vs-typing.

p. 22   *almost 500 billion neurons in our guts:* Melissa Bloom, "Fueling Your Brain: The Correlation between Food & Motivation," EmpowRD Nutrition, May 23, 2021, empowrdnutrition.com/fueling-your-brain-the-correlation -between-food-motivation.

p. 23   *When our brains run low on glucose:* Erik E.J.G. Aller et al., "Starches, Sugars and Obesity," *Nutrients* 3, no. 3 (March 2011): 341–69, doi.org/10.3390/ nu3030341.

p. 23   *Other foods that increase good bacteria in our gut:* Kanti Bhooshan Pandey and Syed Ibrahim Rizvi, "Plant Polyphenols as Dietary Antioxidants in Human Health and Disease," *Oxidative Medicine and Cellular Longevity* 2, no. 5 (November–December 2009): 270-78, doi.org/10.4161/ oxim.2.5.9498; Emiley A. Eloe-Fadrosh et al., "Functional Dynamics of the Gut Microbiome in Elderly People during Probiotic Consumption," *mBio* 6, no. 2 (May 2015): e00231-15, doi.org/10.1128/mbio.00231-15.

4. Behavior: Instincts, Identity, and Choices

p. 40   *high-knowledge, low-assumption environment:* Rita McGrath and Ian MacMillan, "Discovery-Driven Planning," *Harvard Business Review*, July–August 1995, hbr.org/1995/07/discovery-driven-planning.

p. 40   *"What got you here won't get you there":* Marshall Goldsmith with Mark Reiter, *What Got You Here Won't Get You There: How Successful People Become Even More Successful!* (Hyperion, 2007).

p. 45   *An organization's identity is:* Callen Anthony and Mary Tripsas, "Organizational Identity and Innovation," in *The Oxford Handbook of Organizational Identity*, edited by Michael G. Pratt et al. (Oxford University Press, 2016), 418.

p. 45   *a shared understanding of who we are requires:* Anthony and Tripsas, "Organizational Identity," 418.

p. 47   *Over the following decade-plus, Warby Parker:* "Events & Presentations," Warby Parker, 2024, investors.warbyparker.com/events-presentations/ default.aspx; Jason Del Rey, "An Unlikely Startup Enters the Point-of-Sale

Business: Warby Parker," *All Things Digital*, June 24, 2013, allthingsd.com/20130624/an-unlikely-startup-enters-the-point-of -sale-business-warby-parker.

p. 47   *Alessi, an Italian kitchen utensil company:* Violina Rindova, Elena Dalpiaz, and Davide Ravasi, "A Cultural Quest: A Study of Organizational Use of New Cultural Resources in Strategy Formation," *Organization Science* 22, no. 2 (March–April 2011): 413–31, doi.org/10.1287/orsc.1100.0537.

p. 48   *with consistent growth year over year:* Vicente Castellano, "Alessi: Partnering with a Third-Generation Family Business to Rejuvenate an Italian Icon," Oakley Capital, July 12, 2021, oakleycapital.com/ news-and-insights/alessi-partnering-with-a-third-generation-family-business-to-rejuvenate-an-italian-icon.

p. 48   *"can pose major problems for organizations":* Anthony and Tripsas, "Organizational Identity," 425.

p. 48   *research shows that executives tend to do one of three things:* Anthony and Tripsas, "Organizational Identity," 425.

Know Your Innovation Types

p. 57   *Disruptive innovation is a term coined by Harvard professor Clayton Christensen:* "Disruptive Innovation Theory," Christensen Institute, n.d., christenseninstitute.org/theory/disruptive-innovation/.

5. Architecture: Where, Who, and How

p. 60   *distinguishes good strategies from bad strategies:* Jeff Zych, "Notes from 'Good Strategy / Bad Strategy,'" *Jeff Zych's Internet Nook* (blog), June 27, 2018, jlzych.com/2018/06/27/notes-from-good-strategy-bad-strategy.

p. 62   *Google has basically eliminated it:* Christopher Mims, "Google's '20% Time,' Which Brought You Gmail and AdSense, Is Now as Good as Dead," *Quartz*, August 16, 2013, qz.com/115831/googles-20-time-which-brought-you-gmail-and-adsense-is-now-as-good-as-dead.

p. 64   *"it is not the selection of people that determines the degree of exploration:* Alva Taylor and Henrich R. Greve, "Superman or the Fantastic Four? Knowledge Combination and Experience in Innovative Teams," *Academy of Management Journal* 49, no. 4 (August 2006): 723–40, doi.org/10.5465/AMJ.2006.22083029.

p. 64   *"teams that have previously worked together are superior:* Taylor and Greve, "Superman or the Fantastic Four?" Hope's team was pulled from a team she was already managing and who had worked together for years. As a result, they were able to skip critical steps in the team formation phase (storming, norming, etc.) and work together like a well-oiled machine from day one.

p. 64   *Creativity requires outsiders who don't think the way the organization thinks:* Yoonjin Choi, Paul Ingram, and Sang Won Han, "Cultural Breadth and Embeddedness: The Individual Adoption of Organizational Culture as a Determinant of Creativity," *Administrative Science Quarterly* 68, no. 2 (2023): 429–64, doi.org/10.1177/00018392221146792.

p. 64   *"push its boundaries with any nontrivial likelihood of success":* Taylor and Greve, "Superman or the Fantastic Four?"

p. 64   *generalists with broad experience who can connect pieces of knowledge:* Jeff Dyer, Hal Gregersen, and Clayton M. Christensen, *The Innovator's DNA: Mastering the Five Skills of Disruptive Innovators* (Harvard Business Review Press, 2011).

p. 69   *"You don't learn to walk by following the rules:* Peter Economy, "Richard Branson: 19 Inspiring Power Quotes for Success," *Inc.*, March 20, 2015, inc.com/peter-economy/richard-branson-19-inspiring-power-quotes-for-success.html.

p. 69   *Usually, it looks and feels like this:* Damien Newman, "The Process of Design Squiggle," thedesignsquiggle.com.

Know Your Innovation Frameworks

p. 74   *check out the Systemic Design Association:* Systemic Design Association, systemic-design.org.

6. Culture: Toolkit, Team, and Values

p. 81   *"I shall not today attempt further to define:* Justice Potter Stewart quoted in David L. Hudson Jr., "*Jacobellis v. Ohio* (1964)," Free Speech Center, Middle Tennessee State University, last updated July 2, 2024, firstamendment.mtsu.edu/article/jacobellis-v-ohio/.

p. 83   *made two fascinating discoveries:* Boris Groysberg et al., "The Leader's Guide to Corporate Culture," *Harvard Business Review*, January–February 2018, hbr.org/2018/01/the-leaders-guide-to-corporate-culture.

p. 83   *create a matrix against which each of the eight cultures can be plotted:* Graphic adapted from Spencer Stuart, "Culture Alignment Framework," n.d., spencerstuart.com/what-we-do/our-capabilities/leadership-consulting/organizational-culture.

p. 86   *"The founder of an organization simultaneously creates:* Edgar H. Schein, "The Role of the Founder in Creating Organizational Culture," *Organizational Dynamics* 12, no. 1 (Summer 1983): 13–28, doi.org/10.1016/0090-2616(83)90023-2.

8. Behavior: Inspiration and Hard Conversations

p. 108 *"'I don't have time' means 'It's not a priority'"*: Laura Vanderkam, "How to Gain Control of Your Free Time," TED.com, October 2016, 11:44, ted.com/talks/laura_vanderkam_how_to_gain_control_of_your_free_time.

Know Your Decision-Making Models

p. 134 *we use a 4+ decision-making model:* Graphic adapted from Jesse Lyn Stoner, "Four Decision-Making Styles and When to Use Them," *The Gibson Edge*, June 23, 2017, https://www.thegibsonedge.com/blog/four-decision-making-styles-and-when-to-use-them; Judith Stein, "Decision-Making Models," MIT Human Resources, hr.mit.edu/learning-topics/teams/articles/models.

p. 135 *For decisions that fall into the team decision box:* Stein, "Decision-Making Models."

10. Culture: Share, Invite, and Expand

p. 137 *"when one looks at innovation in nature and in culture":* Steven Johnson, *Where Good Ideas Come From: The Natural History of Innovation* (Riverhead, 2010), 22.

p. 138 *In the process of developing an adhesive strong enough:* Information summarized from April Lam, "How Do Sticky Notes Work?" *Science Focus*, Hong Kong University of Science and Technology, sciencefocus.ust.hk/how-do-sticky-notes-work.

p. 138 *Frustrated by bookmarks constantly falling out his hymnal:* Information summarized from "The Invention of the Post-it® Note," National Inventors Hall of Fame, June 5, 2020, invent.org/blog/trends-stem/who-invented-post-it-notes.

12. Behavior: Reflect, Promote, and Repeat

p. 161 *I watched Kenneth Branagh deliver the St. Crispin's Day speech:* Kenneth Branagh, dir., *Henry V* (BBC and Renaissance Films, 1989).

13. Architecture: Challenges, Strategies, and Cynics

p. 174 *"it is the story of every man who:* Victor Hugo, "Villemain," *Things Seen* (*Choses vues*), vol. 1 (George Routledge and Sons, 1887), 88. Available at babel.hathitrust.org/cgi/pt?id=mdp.39015008863600&seq=11.

p. 177 *"view their cynicism as hard-earned wisdom:* Jamil Zaki, "Don't Let Cynicism Undermine Your Workplace," *Harvard Business Review*, September–October 2022, hbr.org/2022/09/dont-let-cynicism-undermine-your-workplace.

p. 177   *70 percent of participants perceived cynics as generally smarter than non-cynics:* Olga Stavrova and Daniel Ehlebracht, "The Cynical Genius Illusion: Exploring and Debunking Lay Beliefs about Cynicism and Competence," *Personality and Social Psychology Bulletin* 45, no. 2 (February 2019): 254–269, doi.org/10.1177/0146167218783195.

p. 178   *cynicism is considered an emotional contagion:* Jeffrey Gaines, "What Is Emotional Contagion Theory? (Definition & Examples)," PositivePsychology.com, February 12, 2021, positivepsychology.com/emotional-contagion.

14. Culture: Movements, Events, and Partners

p. 182   *A movement must be public:* Derek Sivers, "How to Start a Movement," TED.com, February 2010, 2:52, ted.com/talks/derek_sivers_how_to_start_a_movement.

p. 183   *"Innovation theater" is a term coined by Steve Blank:* Steve Blank, "Why Companies Do 'Innovation Theater' Instead of Actual Innovation," *Harvard Business Review*, October 7, 2019, hbr.org/2019/10/why-companies-do-innovation-theater-instead-of-actual-innovation.

p. 188   *most successful hackathon teams spent little time or energy:* Hila Lifshitz-Assaf, Sarah Lebovitz, and Lior Zalmanson, "Minimal and Adaptive Coordination: How Hackathons' Projects Accelerate Innovation without Killing it," *Academy of Management Journal* 64, no. 3 (June 2021): 684–715, doi.org/10.5465/amj.2017.0712.

p. 189   *"to bring order and coherence to the chaotic process:* Lifshitz-Assaf, Lebovitz, and Zalmanson, "Minimal and Adaptive Coordination," 694.

p. 189   *"involved swift sensing and adjusting:* Lifshitz-Assaf, Lebovitz, and Zalmanson, "Minimal and Adaptive Coordination," 698.

p. 191   *"Life moves pretty fast:* John Hughes, dir., *Ferris Bueller's Day Off* (Paramount Pictures, 1986).

p. 191   *main quality shared by all great innovators is:* Jeff Dyer, Hal Gregersen, and Clayton M. Christensen, *The Innovator's DNA: Mastering the Five Skills of Disruptive Innovators* (Harvard Business Press, 2011).

15. One More Thing...

p. 200   *(May I recommend chocolate chip?):* Joanna Gaines, "*Magnolia Table* Chocolate Chip Cookies," *the kitchn*, May 10, 2024, thekitchn.com/joanna-gaines-chocolate-chip-cookies-recipe-257520. To make the cookies gluten-free, use Bob's Red Mill Gluten Free 1-to-1 Baking Flour instead of all-purpose flour. To make the cookies lactose-free, use 8 tablespoons of ghee instead of unsalted butter, and while mixing, drizzle in approximately 2 ounces of coconut milk until the batter is light and fluffy.

PHOTO: LIZ LINDER

About the Author

ROBYN M. BOLTON is the founder and chief navigator at MileZero, a consulting and coaching firm that helps leaders use innovation to confidently and consistently grow business revenue. Robyn is also an assistant professor at the Massachusetts College of Art and Design where she teaches courses in strategy and product innovation in the college's master of design innovation program.

Prior to founding MileZero, she was a partner at Innosight, the innovation and growth strategy consulting firm cofounded by Harvard professor Clayton Christensen, and a manager at the Boston Consulting Group's offices in Boston and Copenhagen.

She began her career at Procter & Gamble as an assistant brand manager on the development and launch of Swiffer and Swiffer WetJet and as brand manager on the Walmart sales team. She earned her MBA at Harvard Business School and graduated from Miami University with a bachelor of science in marketing, cum laude with university honors.

Her articles on innovation have appeared in multiple publications, including *Fast Company*, *Bloomberg Businessweek*, and *Harvard Business Review* online. Her perspectives have been featured in the *New York Times* and NPR's *Marketplace*. She was voted the number one blogger of 2022 and 2023 on human-centered design and innovation.

MileZero is a consulting and coaching firm that helps leaders use innovation to confidently and consistently grow business revenue.

Five core beliefs drive MileZero:

1 Innovation is something different that creates value.

2 Innovation requires curiosity, courage, and commitment.

3 Any organization can innovate, and any person can be an innovator.

4 People (even your customers and your boss) decide with their hearts and justify with their heads.

5 Ideas are a dime a dozen. Decisions are priceless. Action is perfection.

MileZero partners with leaders and their teams to understand their current ABCs of Innovation and develop custom programs that strengthen and accelerate their ABCs while unleashing the power of their innovators to grow and transform the business.

Learn more at **MileZero.io**.

www.ingramcontent.com/pod-product-compliance
Lightning Source LLC
LaVergne TN
LVHW051448090125
800516LV00002B/8